THE WORLD IS VERTICAL

ALSO BY ABISHUR PRAKASH

Next Geopolitics: The Future of World Affairs (Technology) Volume One

Next Geopolitics: The Future of World Affairs (Technology) Volume Two

Go.AI (Geopolitics of Artificial Intelligence)

The Age of Killer Robots

THE WORLD IS VERTICAL

How Technology Is Remaking Globalization

ABISHUR PRAKASH

Center for Innovating the Future

Center for Innovating the Future, Inc

Headquartered in Toronto, Canada

innovatingfuture.com

Library and Archives Canada

Prakash, Abishur

The World Is Vertical: How Technology Is Remaking Globalization

Center for Innovating the Future

ISBN 978-0-9811821-7-9 (hardcover) – ISBN 978-0-9811821-8-6 (paperback) – ISBN 978-0-9811821-9-3 (ebook)

CONTENTS

THE WORLD IS VERTICAL

INTRODUCTION

Welcome To The Vertical World

During a secret meeting in August 1941, the seeds of modern-day globalization were laid down. As World War II ravaged Europe and Asia, the leaders of the US and United Kingdom secretly met off the coast of Canada. They met to discuss what is known today as the "Atlantic Charter." The charter was a blueprint for the world after the war ended and the allies won. In the charter were eight principles, like liberalizing world trade and international standards for labor and economy. The Western powers knew that the world could not withstand another war. The global economy was in ruins, and nuclear weapons were being developed. The only way to protect the world was to redesign it. This crisis led to the creation of new rules and protocols that integrated nations. The US, UK, and their allies established a new structure for the world in which countries acted in unison and became dependent on one another for success. Since then, governments around the world have adopted the principles in the Atlantic Charter. These governments joined the same institutions to manage international affairs (e.g., United Nations, World Trade Organization). They adopted the same trade rules to grow the economy (e.g., free trade, removing tariffs and taxes). They built the same immigration systems to attract people, businesses, and ideas (e.g., points-based, special visas). They used the same gateways to oversee their financial systems (e.g., SWIFT, reserve currencies). They enlisted the same technologies to propel their societies forward (e.g., the Internet, telecommunications).

As nations were woven together like threads, globalization took off, leading to uniformity in how the world worked. It was clear what direction the world was moving in (i.e., more connectivity, more integration). By integrating the world, barriers and walls that once divided nations were knocked down. The world became open and accessible. Areas like governance and economy, which were once the purview of individual governments, were now influenced by the whole world (i.e., global governance, global economy). Instead of a handful of developed nations (or colonial powers) operating in isolation from everyone else, globalization connected everybody. Most importantly, globalization promised everybody an equal playing field. And, at the outset, globalization appeared to be working. The iPhone, while designed in Silicon Valley, was built on the back of globalization. From Japan (Bluetooth hardware) to Italy (power management component) to Germany (network pieces) to Taiwan (accelerometers) to China (assembly), the iPhone represented how businesses could benefit from a deeply integrated world. Or take "M-Pesa," a mobile payment app used in Kenya for people without a bank account. The app was developed by Vodafone (the United Kingdom) for Samsung and Transsion phones (South Korea and China) powered by telecommunications networks controlled by Airtel (India). M-Pesa succeeded because societies and economies had become accessible to one another.

As globalization accelerated, the world was becoming "borderless." And, it appeared that nations were in alignment with how the world was changing. Except, behind the scenes, this was not the case. The design of the world was no longer working for many nations. These nations were becoming angry for several reasons. First, governments felt some economies benefited from globalization more than others (i.e., American businesses outsourcing millions of jobs to India because they could quickly move them). Second, the institutions that governed the world struggled to balance the role of advanced nations with the appetite of emerging powers (i.e., climate accords failing as China and the US pointed fingers at each other). Third, a handful of nations had reached a point where they no longer wanted to follow the rules set by "someone else" (i.e., BRICS vs. G7). Fourth, when a global crisis emerged, the integration of the world was viewed as a risk (i.e., selling of "toxic stocks" on Wall Street fueling a global recession). Fifth, and lastly, some governments were flaunting the rules, resulting in nations saying, "if they can do that, then so can I" (i.e., Iran offering "oil for goods" as a way to skirt sanctions).

These challenges caused nations to question and criticize globalization. Except, even though governments may have felt globalization was not working, there was no alternative. Countries were stuck. For instance, since their first meeting in 2009, the BRIC (Brazil, Russia, India, and China) nations - later BRICS after South Africa joined in 2011 - have met every year. But, they still have not developed an alternative to the Western systems beyond ideas. And, climate accords, like the Paris Climate Agreement, while global in nature, have ultimately always depended on a few nations playing ball (like the US, India, and China), making the rest of the world dependent on those powers.

That is, until now.

As the chorus to move away from globalization grows louder, something unexpected has begun. The emergence of technologies like artificial intelligence (AI), blockchain, robotics, and 5G, is giving rise to a new design for the world. Nations are using these technologies to reclaim the sovereignty they feel they have lost because of globalization. Through these technologies, governments are establishing an independent presence in the world. They no longer depend on the traditional global protocols, ideals, and systems. These technologies are tools that are giving nations a new voice. And, with this voice, countries are questioning the status quo like never before, such as why are they using someone else's currency, ecosystems, platforms, services, or software? And why they cannot develop alternatives? These technologies allow nations to walk away from globalization and chart a new, independent path for themselves.

Instead of the world staying open and accessible, it is becoming closed, restricted, and full of technology-based walls and barriers. The world is becoming vertical. Technology is ending globalization in its current form and is giving rise to a new design for the world. As countries act vertically, they are discarding the systems that have integrated the world for decades.

There are many drivers of the vertical world. One of them is the competition between the US and China. To displace the US as the world's leader, China is betting big on technology. The Chinese have developed technology services and platforms that could take control of the world away from the US. To stop this, the US is building walls that block out Chinese technology. In response, China is building its own barriers that limit what the US can do. Both sides are trying to contain each other through technology. As the US and China use technology this way, nations are picking sides, causing the world to split.

Another driver of the vertical world is new, exclusive institutions. Instead of nations turning to traditional institutions, like the United Nations (UN), to govern the world, governments are creating new technology-based institutions like "D10." This institution is a grouping of ten democracies to set the rules for 5G. Except, D10 is not open to everyone. It is exclusive, consisting of only like-minded nations. As governments form new institutions, the world is dividing into camps. These camps are competing to set the technology rules for the world. The era when a specific issue (like trade) was dealt with by a single institution (like the World Trade Organization) is ending. Now, multiple institutions are emerging to deal with the same technology issues. And, equally challenging, a single nation, like Australia or Israel, may be members of one or more of these technology-based institutions, led by competing powers. Does this promote integration or the complete opposite? The time when every nation followed the same rules and structures is passing. The time when nations looked to globalization as a way to move forward is concluding. Instead of countries operating in unison, because of technology, they are increasingly operating in variance. Quite literally, the same forces that have been driving globalization are now also driving the vertical world.

This book is a story about how the vertical world is taking shape. It looks at how technology is causing the world to divide, split, and fracture at almost every level. The vertical world goes far beyond the US-China competition or the formation of new institutions. It is about the new geography of the world, a new reality for humanity, and a new status quo for businesses. The first chapter looks at how Europe is establishing new borders. The second chapter looks at how Saudi Arabia is dividing the Middle East. The third chapter looks at how India is fighting against future colonialism. The fourth chapter looks at how South Korea is reasserting its place in the world. The fifth chapter looks at how Russia is walling itself off from other nations. The sixth chapter looks at how the US and China are splitting the world. The seventh chapter looks at Japan's new independence. The eighth and final chapter looks at Israel's journey towards self-sufficiency. The vertical world has no limits to who it will affect and how. As new technology-based fault lines emerge, everybody's place in the world is being reconfigured.

When the seeds of modern-day globalization were planted in the 20th century, the world was in chaos. Only a few nations had power. Consensus and colonialism ushered in a new design for the world. Globalization promised nations a path to success, but this promise fell short. Now, an uprising is taking place. Countries of all shapes and sizes are tired of the current design. The drums of war may not be beating, but the rumblings of change are becoming stronger.

Nations are wielding technology to enforce global change regardless if anyone else wants it or approves. Through technology, the strings of globalization, which have woven the world together, are being untied. A new manifesto is being written. The biggest decision facing nations and businesses is whether they will chain themselves to a slowing axis that has spun the world for decades. Or, whether they will leap towards a world that is rapidly becoming vertical. In either case, if leaders take too long to decide, technology will choose for them.

CHAPTER ONE

The New Borders Of Europe

For decades, Europe has driven globalization. The de facto steward of the region, the European Union (EU), operated with one goal: integrate European nations by removing barriers to trade and movement of people. This model gave birth to a single currency and open borders. It turned the EU into one of the largest economies in the world. And, because of the EU's economic weight, whatever the EU did affected Europe as a whole – even non-EU members.

Except, as Europe operated this way, European nations lost their sovereignty. On the world stage, Europe became dominated by the US, Russia, and parts of the Indo-Pacific. And, internally, European governments started to feel that their needs and desires were either drowned out by louder voices, more voices, or outright ignored. A new, uncomfortable reality was settling in for the continent. Besides a few key areas, like manufacturing or finance, the world was quietly moving on without Europe. Perhaps, European leaders knew this was happening. But, because there was no way out, they eagerly awaited the moment when they could take action.

Now, with technology, that moment has arrived. The "old model" of Europe is gone. On multiple levels, Europe is splitting because of technology. On the world stage, the United Kingdom, having left the EU, is presenting the world with its vertical ideas for technology. Meanwhile, the EU, concerned about the rise of China and the dominance of US technology, is reasserting its borders. At the same time, within Europe itself, divisions are emerging as European nations take steps around technology that differ from one another.

The way Europe has operated for decades is suddenly losing steam. The paradigm of integration and removing barriers is no longer attractive. Governments are challenging the idea that the only way to succeed is by working together. A new type of hunger for sovereignty is driving European nations. To reclaim their power and create a new role for themselves globally, they are turning to technology.

The United Kingdom Blocks China

In June 2016, the United Kingdom (UK) voted to leave the EU. Since then, all eyes have been on how "Brexit" (British exit) may divide Europe from commerce to immigration. Few, if any, have been paying attention to the impact that Brexit is having on technology. Like most things, the area seldom looked at is where the most activity is taking place. At its core, technology is keeping the spirit of Brexit alive. It is allowing the UK to not only walk away from the EU but globalization too. The nation that helped create the current design of the world is now challenging it. The UK is using technology to wall itself off from China. This choice is a different path for the UK. In the past, it opened itself up to China, seeking to become China's gateway into Europe. Today, however, the UK has a different attitude. As China uses the current design of the world to build its power, the UK is taking radical steps to counter that.

The UK's actions are sending a message to other nations: globalization will only be supported if certain countries, like the UK, remain in charge. If that does not happen, then the vertical world will be quickly ushered in. In July 2020, the UK announced a ban on Huawei's 5G technology, requiring British telecommunications companies to remove the Chinese technology from their networks by 2027.[i] By banning Huawei's 5G, the UK has established a new wall between itself and China. A critical Chinese technology has been locked out of the UK. Before targeting Huawei's 5G, the UK took another step towards restricting China. In May 2020, the UK announced a new group called "D10," which stands for ten democracies. The group, made up of nations like India, Australia, Japan, and the US, is establishing the global rules for technologies like 5G.

This new technology-focused institution is a double whammy. First, D10 is a direct shot at Chinese 5G. It represents a new camp of nations attempting to lock out Chinese technology from their markets. But, second, and more importantly, to take on China, the UK is not turning to institutions like the UN or World Trade

Organization (WTO), which have governed the world for decades. Instead, to deal with the rise of China, the UK has launched a new technology-focused institution made up of only a few like-minded nations. And, D10 is not the only new institution forming. In the same month that the UK announced D10, the US joined the "Global Partnership on AI (GPAI)," a G7-led group building the global rules for AI. Like with D10, China was not invited to GPAI. New institutions are being formed that exclude much of the world and take aim at specific nations and technologies. This is dividing the world along new fault lines. And, tomorrow, D10 may not be alone in setting the global technology rules. Other nations might join hands to build their own institutions and technology practices. In the coming years, multiple institutions may exist, and may compete, to develop technology rules that other nations adopt.

The UK is also building new barriers that limit how people move. In October 2020, the UK proposed limits on what certain international students can study.[ii] Specifically, the government wants to stop Chinese students from studying subjects like cybersecurity and aerospace. The UK is worried that Chinese students studying in the country could steal high-level intellectual property (IP). Or that these students may take their new education back to China to start competitive companies that outcompete Britain on the world stage. Restricting international students because of geopolitics is a massive change in British thinking. For decades, the UK supported the movement of people and ideas around the world. Now, when it comes to technology, the UK is striking a different tone. This proposal, to limit what certain ethnicities can study, fundamentally challenges the British and Western ethos. It means that the core ideals, like accessibility and equal opportunity, are now being redefined because of the vertical world.

The UK is also taking action against foreign investment and acquisitions of British technology. The UK does not want China to dominate its economy. In November 2020, the UK announced new measures to prevent takeovers of firms in critical sectors like AI, robotics, quantum computing, and space.[iii] The UK is worried that certain Chinese investments/acquisitions could threaten British competitiveness. While governments have constantly scrutinized foreign investment, they have been reluctant to limit investment from "economic superpowers." For example, in December 2016, after the Iran Deal had been signed,

Iran's state airline signed a deal to purchase Boeing planes. [iv] In other words, even after years of bitter relations, when the US offered foreign investment, Iran took it. Except, with China, it is a different story. The UK does not want its future economy to be tied to China. By introducing the new rules for foreign investment, the UK is erecting a new "wall" around British technology that blocks out China.

The EU Throws US Technology Out

Over the past several years, the EU has begun challenging the US. Instead of allowing US technology to dominate, the EU has started taking steps to remove US technology from the continent. A new line of thinking has emerged: why does the EU need US technology? This attitude is giving rise to European technology that matches what the US has been offering. As the European technology emerges, new barriers are forming, limiting the role that US technology plays in Europe. One area where this is taking place is with cloud computing. In June 2020, France and Germany launched "Gaia-X." This is a project to build a local system for European data to be stored and shared. It does not depend on the US (or

China). [v] The hope is that, through Gaia-X, new European industries and companies will be created that can supply the services that Europe's people and businesses need. Why does Europe want to move away from US-driven cloud computing? Part of it has to do with data. In March 2018, the US passed the "Clarifying Lawful Overseas Use of Data Act," or as it is more commonly referred to, the "CLOUD Act." [vi] This act allows the US government to request data on servers of American companies. The massive amounts of European data accessed by Washington is a huge threat (and has been for several years). Except, data is only one part of the equation. The other part is that Europe does not want its future to be tied to US technology like in the past. From servers to software, by taking control of European cloud computing, the EU is gaining control of a sector that has been entirely dominated by the US. By controlling cloud computing, the US ensured that the world, including its allies like the EU, remained dependent on it. As the EU builds its cloud computing infrastructure, Europe will depend on European technology, removing the US from the equation. In fact, some of Washington's closest allies in Europe have been wanting to replace US technology, even before Gaia-X.

In September 2019, Germany said it wanted to enhance its "digital sovereignty." To achieve this, it would stop using services from US technology companies like Microsoft.[vii]

Another way that Europe is pushing out US technology is with AI. In April 2018, scientists in Europe unveiled a new project to build AI labs called the "European Lab for Learning and Intelligent System" or "ELLIS."[viii] The idea was to stop AI talent from leaving Europe for the US and China. ELLIS was modeled on CERN, the particle collider created after World War II to stop physics experts from leaving Europe. In December 2019, Europe officially launched ELLIS, putting aside US$220 million and building AI labs in several cities, like Amsterdam, Copenhagen, and Zurich, along with Tel Aviv (Israel was the only non-European nation to join ELLIS).[ix] However, ELLIS goes against a critical tenet of the EU: open borders. Until recently, the EU did not restrict the movement of people, including between Europe and the US (or parts of the Indo-Pacific). Now, because of how AI could grow economies, the EU is building indirect walls. Through AI labs, the EU is beginning to take a stand: incentivizing certain people to stay in Europe and not go overseas. ELLIS represents a new attempt to control where European AI talent goes and who it benefits.

The EU is also challenging US technology with antitrust and anti-monopoly charges. European regulators want to bring US technology firms under their thumb. And, indirectly, create European alternatives to these firms. For example, in July 2017, Google was fined US$2.7 billion by the European Commission for antitrust violations. The fine targeted Google's shopping services and how Google's products were benefitting from search algorithms.[x] Since 2017, the European Commission has issued US$9.7 billion in fines against Google alone.[xi] In May 2017, Facebook was fined US$122 million by the European regulator over its acquisition of the messaging service "WhatsApp."[xii] In September 2018, European regulators looked into fining Facebook up to US$1.63 billion for a data breach.[xiii] In December 2019, the European Commission began investigating Facebook's data collection practices resulting in Facebook suing regulators in July 2020.[xiv] The EU is scrutinizing even new technology initiatives by US companies. In August 2019, as Facebook marketed its new digital currency, "Libra," antitrust concerns were raised in Europe, prompting an investigation into the currency.[xv] By imposing these kinds of fines, the EU is making it more and more difficult for US technology firms to operate on the continent freely.

At the same time, Europe is looking at introducing a digital tax, another attack on US technology firms, drawing a rebuke from the US. In June 2020, the US walked out of talks with the EU on a digital tax[xvi], resulting in top EU officials saying they would embark on a digital tax without assistance in 2021.[xvii] But, individual EU states are not waiting for a bloc-wide digital tax. In July 2019, France approved its own "digital services tax" that targeted large technology firms. One of these firms was Amazon. In August 2019, Amazon said it would pass along the tax to French sellers on its platform, putting the French government in an awkward position.[xviii] However, in January 2020, after the US imposed sanctions on French goods, France halted its digital tax initiative until further notice.[xix] Like fines, a digital tax represents a new way to restrict how US technology reaches European consumers and businesses.

Instead of being open and accessible, the European landscape is becoming hostile and restrictive for US companies in some cases. All of these measures point to the EU thinking vertically. The EU is actively creating technology-based barriers that make it difficult for US technology firms to succeed in Europe. And, as the EU takes these steps, it is quickly building services that replace what the US has been selling. The US-EU alliance, built on globalization, is now being challenged. The EU is drawing new borders through technology that defines where the US ends and where the EU begins.

A European Disunion

The vertical world is also leading to massive internal division within the EU. One area where this is happening is biotechnology. In July 2018, the European Parliament, the elected body representing all EU members, approved new legislation called the "GMO (Genetically Modified Organism) Directive." [xx] This allowed EU members to ban the cultivation and importation of GMO crops. And, the ban extended to gene-edited crops, a type of crop manipulation that is not traditionally considered GMO. Except, in October 2018, the Dutch government took a stand. It parted ways with the European Parliament, saying that it may begin developing genetically modified crops. [xxi] On biotechnology, the control that the EU once had is starting to diminish. Instead of following the EU's rules, nations like the Netherlands are deciding what to do independently. By ignoring the EU on biotechnology, the Netherlands has established a new barrier limiting the EU's jurisdiction. No longer are EU directives carried out without question.

There is also division emerging because of the lack of EU leadership. In February 2019, Austria called on the European Commission to rule whether a nation can use Chinese 5G technology.[xxii] But, no ruling was made. Lack of leadership is dividing the EU as countries allow opposing 5G technology. While Sweden, Poland, Romania, and Bulgaria have all banned Chinese 5G technology, other EU members have not. As of November 2020, EU members like France, Germany, Italy, Spain, the Netherlands, Norway, and Finland had not banned Huawei (or ZTE) from their 5G networks. A new split is emerging in the EU. Some nations are using European or American 5G technology, while others are using - or are open to using - Chinese 5G technology. In other words, because the EU is not leading on 5G rules, EU members are taking matters into their own hands. Some European nations are cozying up to China (by allowing Huawei), while others are cozying up to the US (by excluding Huawei). EU members are moving in different directions, challenging how "unified" the EU is.

The future European defense strategies are also divided. Until recently, the EU had a single defense doctrine, influenced mainly by the North Atlantic Treaty Organization (NATO). But, now, EU members are acting independently to deal with new challenges like space. In July 2019, France announced that it would be launching its space force. Part of this means that the next-generation French satellites will have offensive capabilities like lasers. [xxiii] But, in the same month, Germany said it did not want EU members, like France, to go at it alone in space, and instead, the bloc should be using organizations like the European Space Agency (ESA). [xxiv] When it comes to space defense, the EU is going vertical. France is seeking an independent space force, while Germany wants a pan-European force.

There is also NATO, who in October 2020 announced it would be establishing its own "space command" to protect the satellites of NATO members.[xxv] And, that the new command would be based in Germany. Alongside this, in January 2019, an EU minister called for creating a European space force independent of NATO.[xxvi] How many space forces will there be in Europe? Instead of one representing the whole EU, there may be several. France is preparing its space force. Germany wants a European space force but is also becoming the headquarters of a NATO space force. And others in the EU want a separate space force from NATO. As EU members invest in space technologies, they are realizing that they no longer need (or want) each other the way they once did. They are unplugging from the old model in ways that could be difficult to reverse.

There is also division when it comes to digital currencies. In October 2020, the European Central Bank (ECB) said that it would look into launching a "Digital Euro."[xxvii] Before this, in May 2020, the Bank of France held a successful trial with a Digital Euro, marking the first time the digital currency was used in Europe.[xxviii] Except, while the EU moves forward with a Digital Euro, a handful of EU states are developing their own sovereign digital currencies. In January 2018, Poland announced it was creating its own national digital currency[xxix], and in October 2020, Estonia unveiled it was looking into developing its own digital currency for the economy.[xxx] Besides the free movement of people, nothing has unified the EU more than its single currency (the Euro). Now, in the vertical world, this is at risk. Nations do not want to give a single European central bank control over their economies. With technology, European governments are taking back this control. At the same time, the "economic weight" that the EU once used to make Europe operate a certain way is being threatened by technology. Nations are no longer intimidated or worried they will lose out if they walk away.

Conclusion

The nations of Europe have gone full circle. Decades ago, they helped create the design of the world. Then, on this design, they expanded and grew. Now, they have returned to this design, ready to replace it with something very vertical. Instead of being open and accessible, Europe is becoming full of technology-based walls and barriers. On the world stage, nations like the US and China are being forced to rethink how they grow their footprints in Europe. Internally, countries like the Netherlands and France are using technology to reconfigure their relationship with the rest of the union. And, alongside this, nations like the UK, independent of the rest of Europe, are using technology to establish a new, vertical way of connecting with the world. The goal of integration is no longer a priority for Europe. Now, the goal of becoming sovereign is at the forefront.

Because of technology, the Europe that the world has known for decades is disappearing. The unity and commonality that existed before are gone. Now, the Europe that is forming is governed by the individual ambitions of nations, not the collective whole. As European countries wall themselves off, internally and externally, globalization will lose one of its most important allies. The weight of carrying globalization forward will fall on other governments who may have a different idea of who globalization should serve. But, most importantly, if nations with a shared history, who have operated in a globalized way for centuries, can suddenly depart from the old design because of technology, nobody is untouchable in the vertical world.

Just as Europe's integration was once a model for the world, Europe's new division may also serve as a model. After all, if European nations can still achieve success when they are divided from one another or the world, then many other countries may start to question just how necessary globalization is for their future as well.

CHAPTER TWO

A Divided Middle East

Globalization has been a challenge for the Middle East. First, history and religion were "barriers" stopping the Middle East from becoming open and accessible. Any idea of integrating or thinking collectively was met with hesitation or rejection. Second, ideas from the West were traditionally viewed as a threat to Middle Eastern beliefs. And, globalization was an idea conceived by the West. Except, there was one area where the

Middle East discarded this thinking: oil. After Middle Eastern countries discovered oil, the region had to buy into globalization. To effectively sell oil to the world, Middle Eastern nations had to work together and integrate their economies. For the first time, barriers were brought down (or overlooked), and there was some unity.

The visible force driving this transformation was Saudi Arabia. The government in Riyadh used oil to create a new "structure" for the region. And, in the process, Saudi Arabia became the region's leader. From oil output to foreign policy, Saudi Arabia called the shots. But, this structure was fragile. It depended on oil holding its value. If oil were to lose its value, the structure that held parts of the Middle East together would fall apart. And Saudi Arabia's power would be threatened.

This collapse of power is what is taking place today.

As oil loses its value (demand), the structure of the Middle East is cracking. Now, Saudi Arabia is thinking differently. It is betting on technology to fuel the economy and replace oil. As Saudi Arabia adopts the new thinking, it is walking away from the old structure built on globalization. Unlike oil, which required Saudi Arabia to integrate, Saudi Arabia can operate independently when it comes to technology. Technology is giving Saudi Arabia a new axis to stand on that does not require globalization to succeed. And, as Saudi Arabia moves in this direction, Middle Eastern nations are going their separate ways. The unity and alignment that once existed in the region are now disappearing because of technology. The old hesitations and fears in the Middle East that countries overcame by selling oil, are now being amplified by technology. As the most powerful nation in the region eyes technology, the design of the Middle East is becoming vertical.

The Arab World Splits

In the Arab world, the two most powerful nations are Saudi Arabia and the United Arab Emirates (UAE). In the past, these two nations worked together. Now, when it comes to technology, they are starting to compete. This new competition is beginning to split the Arab world. One area of the competition is over technology companies. In January 2021, Saudi Arabia announced a new project called "Programme HQ" to attract various companies, such as those in the technology sectors, from Dubai to Riyadh.[xxxi] Shortly after the Saudi announcement, the UAE announced a new program called "Moonshot 2071," which seeks to attract the most talented graduates in the world to build the UAE's future.[xxxii] A new battle is being waged. Saudi Arabia wants to poach talent and investment from the UAE. And, at the same time, the UAE seeks to attract key technology talent away from Saudi Arabia. For the first time, Saudi Arabia and the UAE are competing for the same resources (i.e., talent and investment). This competition represents a new barrier between Saudi Arabia and the UAE. Instead of working together, as they did with oil, they are competing when it comes to technology. The more these nations compete over technology, the less they will integrate. In the race to design their economies around new vectors, Saudi Arabia and the UAE are putting globalization on hold.

As Saudi Arabia and the UAE compete, it will lead to a new future for businesses. Unlike in the past, when companies viewed Saudi Arabia and the UAE as one, going forward, companies will look at them as two competing economies. Instead of investing in Saudi Arabia or the UAE to access the whole Arab world, businesses may soon be investing to access that specific nation, forcing some companies to pick sides. At the same time, government investments overseas could soon be suspended. Over the past several years, Saudi Arabia has emerged as a significant investor in the UAE, especially in real estate. Going forward, Saudi Arabia could halt investments if they are indirectly helping the UAE's technology sector (and vice versa). The government policies of the past, which have influenced relations between Saudi Arabia and the UAE, may quickly be rewritten because of the vertical world.

Another area where the Arab world is splitting is space. In July 2014, the UAE announced it was planning a mission to Mars.[xxxiii] In November 2020, the UAE launched this mission, sending a probe to study the Martian atmosphere. In February 2021, a space probe named "Al Amal" began to orbit Mars.[xxxiv] The UAE proved that, with vision, any nation could become a space power. But, the mission was significant for another reason: it was the first such mission for the entire Arab world. And, it took place with Saudi Arabia in the shadows. Until recently, it was Saudi Arabia that took the "big steps." Except, through space, the UAE had shown it could also lead the Arab world. Of course, Saudi Arabia was not going to be left behind. In December 2018, the government in Riyadh established a Saudi space agency.[xxxv] And, in October 2020, Saudi Arabia unveiled US$2.1 billion in funding for its space strategy.[xxxvi] Even in space, Saudi Arabia and the UAE are not aligned. They are diverging from each other. Like with the battle over technology companies, both sides are taking steps in space that lead to competition and new barriers. But, in space, the barriers are not just between Saudi Arabia and the UAE. They will soon affect the whole Arab world. For example, the UAE is developing its own navigation system, independent of the rest of the world. In August 2020, the UAE said it would be launching its first navigation satellite in 2021.[xxxvii] Will Saudi Arabia use the UAE's navigation system? Or, will Saudi Arabia launch its own to compete with the UAE? In space, the Arab world could face a new dilemma: who will they follow? When it comes to technology, Arab nations may have to choose who they want to revolve around: the UAE or Saudi Arabia. And, as Arab countries pick sides, the Arab world will increasingly become vertical.

On the geopolitical front, the Arab world is already fracturing. In September 2020, the UAE established full diplomatic relations with Israel. In the backdrop of the UAE-Israel agreement was technology. In July 2020, both sides agreed to cooperate around AI and cloud computing to fight Covid-19. [xxxviii] In other words, technology had built a foundation for the UAE and Israel to change their relationship in a dramatic way. Except, most importantly, the UAE took this step without Saudi Arabia. Just a short time ago, Saudi Arabia would have led the Arab world in redesigning geopolitics. But, with Israel, the situation played out differently. Technology had allowed the UAE to act independently, without anyone else. Even so, Saudi Arabia had its own strategy. In November 2020, the prime minister of Israel allegedly traveled to Saudi Arabia to meet with the Saudi leadership.[xxxix] They met in NEOM, a US$500 billion megacity in the northwestern region of Saudi Arabia, governed by emerging technologies. A critical link between Saudi Arabia and the UAE - geopolitics - has been severed by technology. While Saudi Arabia and the UAE are moving in the same direction (better relations with Israel), they do so without working with each other. Equally important, technology allowed Saudi Arabia to take a less "globalized" approach to normalizing ties with Israel. Instead of using the traditional institutions, like the UN, Saudi Arabia used its technology-driven megacity to reset relations with Israel. Instead of turning to globalization, Saudi Arabia turned away and used NEOM.

There are also future areas where the split between Saudi Arabia and the UAE may expand. One of them is gene editing. In November 2017, the city of Abu Dhabi unveiled a police plan for 2057. Alongside robotic police on streets and a police station in space, there is also a plan to have "genomic police."[xl] These are police that could penalize and punish people for manipulating their genes a certain way. Except, in Saudi Arabia, there has been no formal ruling on gene editing. Suppose the government in Riyadh outright bans gene editing, as it has done with human cloning[xli], while the UAE allows it (with specific laws). In that case, it means that there may be no alignment between Saudi Arabia and the UAE even in future areas. Both sides may rule differently, making the public policy around emerging technologies a new kind of division in the Arab world.

Saudi Arabia and the UAE are moving in opposite directions when it comes to future technologies. This competition, between the two most powerful nations in the region, is breaking the structure of the Arab world. Instead of the Arab world operating as one, led by a single power, it is splitting into different sides. Instead of a single Arab world, soon, there may be multiple, each revolving around a different power. And, through technology, each of these mini-worlds may clash and compete with one another to lead the region.

A New, Saudi Currency Emerges

The adoption of common currencies has been a driving force for globalization. One of the main ways this adoption happened was by pricing oil, a commodity that every nation needed, a certain way. And behind this was a deal struck by the US and Saudi Arabia. After the US stepped away from the gold standard in the 1970s, it signed an agreement to have Saudi Arabia sell all oil in US dollars. This deal gave birth to what is known today as the "PetroDollar." On the back of the PetroDollar, the entire world began to buy and sell all forms of energy in US dollars. The PetroDollar not only gave the US a tremendous amount of power over the world, but it also integrated the global economy along a new, common vector. Everyone was using US dollars to buy and sell energy. Now, Saudi Arabia is stepping away from this model. In December 2017, Saudi Arabia and the UAE announced they would be developing a new digital currency to settle cross-border trade.[xlii] In February 2019, the two nations trialed the new currency called "Aber."[xliii] This is the paradox of the vertical world. In some areas, like attracting companies or space missions, Saudi Arabia and the UAE are competing with each other. But, in other areas, like digital currencies, both nations are collaborating and integrating further.

The new digital currency will give Saudi Arabia more control over how it sells to the world. Instead of using the US dollar for oil sales, Saudi Arabia could soon use Aber, ending the PetroDollar agreement. Digital currencies could act as a new barrier, restricting how globalized some currencies can be. Certain currencies, like the US dollar, may lose ground in certain nations as local digital currencies, like Aber, are adopted. In fact, Saudi Arabia could incentivize countries to purchase oil in Aber. This is what Venezuela tried in the past. In December 2017, Venezuela launched a new digital currency called "Petro" to sell oil and skirt US sanctions.[xliv] One of the first nations Venezuela approached was India, offering a 30% price reduction if New Delhi bought oil in Petro.[xlv] Aber may also create a domino effect in the Middle East as more nations ditch the US dollar. Saudi Arabia could take Aber to other

Middle Eastern countries, offering them a way to become more independent. Arab governments, long cautious about adopting anything Western, might jump at a local, Arab-controlled currency that keeps financial power in the region. Or, other Middle Eastern nations, inspired by what Saudi Arabia has done with Aber, may choose to build their own digital currencies from scratch.

The emergence of multiple digital currencies in the Middle East could create new walls between nations. Governments may pressure one another to settle trade in their digital currency. And, in the process, sovereign digital currencies will put many foreign currencies under siege. Digital currencies could also divide the Middle East dominated-forums. For example, the Organization of the Petroleum Exporting Countries (OPEC) may become paralyzed as members clash over what digital currency to price oil in and how this affects oil output. Or, the Gulf Cooperation Council (GCC) may become divided as different members pitch their own digital currency to the rest of the group. The next era of division in the Middle East could revolve around how nations are reclaiming sovereignty by ditching global currencies and using local, digital currencies. At the same time, radical steps by Saudi Arabia towards the US dollar may push other governments to challenge the US in new ways through technology. After all, if Saudi Arabia, one of America's closest allies, can act vertically, then so can the whole world.

Saudi Arabia Takes Control Of Its Defense

Over the past several decades, another force that has driven Saudi Arabia's integration with the world has been defense. Because of shared geopolitical concerns, many Arab nations have been unified by defense, meaning they have put the US in charge of their security. Defense has deepened Saudi Arabia's role in the globalized world. As Saudi Arabia exported energy, other nations offered protection to secure that energy. Except, this made Saudi Arabia dependent on other countries for defense, a position most governments do not want to be in. Now, the government in Riyadh has begun taking steps to take back control. The catalyst for this is China. As relations between Saudi Arabia and China have grown over the years, mainly through oil trade, new areas of cooperation have emerged, including defense. In March 2017, China signed US$65 billion worth of deals in Saudi Arabia, including building a factory to produce the Chinese CH-4 drone (which competes with US military drones).[xlvi] It was the third such factory in the world, after similar drone facilities in Pakistan and Myanmar. And, in November 2019, Saudi Arabia began discussions on a separate drone deal, this time to import "killer drones" from Ziyan, a Chinese drone firm.[xlvii] As China develops advanced defense technologies, it is adopting a different model. Instead of manufacturing defense products at home, China is making these products in other nations, like Saudi Arabia. And, as this happens, Saudi Arabia may end up developing its own defense industry.

By building the next-generation defense products for China, Saudi Arabia is transitioning from being an importer of defense equipment to a producer and possibly, an exporter. It is acquiring expertise that it could use to build its own defense industries. In fact, this may already have happened. In January 2020, Saudi Arabia announced it was developing its own system to fight off enemy drones.[xlviii] And, in April 2020, Saudi Arabia announced it would begin manufacturing its own, homegrown drone systems in 2021.[xlix] As Saudi Arabia builds its own defense industries, a new source of division could emerge in the world. At one level, Saudi Arabia is enabling China to compete with the likes of the US, Russia, the United Kingdom, and Israel when it comes to defense. China is now producing advanced defense products for the world. Nations now have multiple options for their next-generation military needs. But, at another level, Saudi Arabia is accelerating the localization of defense. Localizing defense is similar to what India has been doing. The government in New Delhi has been demanding that defense firms who want to sell to the Indian armed forces produce their offerings in India itself (also known as "Make in India"). Nations like Saudi Arabia and India are building local defense industries that reduce their dependency on the rest of the world. When governments can localize defense, they no longer need the established powers (or structures) like they once did.

Alongside this, Saudi Arabia may export its defense know-how. Just as South Korea exports smart cities, Saudi Arabia may soon export ready-to-go defense industries to regional allies. The more Saudi Arabia exports its defense expertise, the more governments will begin approaching defense through a vertical lens. And, as Saudi Arabia takes back control of defense, it will be able to deal with geopolitics more independently. The government in Riyadh may take steps alone that it once relied on other nations for. This further divides the Middle East. It means that Saudi Arabia could take military steps, through technology, that the rest of the region (or the world) may not be comfortable with or support. Except, unlike in the past, when Saudi Arabia may have paused a decision to win back support - like going after Qatar - now it may not care.

Conclusion

The vertical world is ushering in a new future for Saudi Arabia. As demand for oil shrinks, Saudi Arabia is no longer chasing globalization. Through technology, Saudi Arabia is beginning to act independently and build new barriers between itself and the rest of the world. This is resulting in a massive change. The Middle East, which has revolved around Saudi Arabia for decades, is splitting. In the vertical world, neighbors like the UAE are being looked at as new competitors. And, global allies like the US are being replaced. What is unexpected in all this is how aggressively Saudi Arabia is willing to replace its old source of power (oil) with new power (technology). This is a risk and a big bet. Instead of using the tried and tested model, Saudi Arabia is innovating its future. For example, the megacity NEOM spans three nations (Saudi Arabia, Egypt, and Jordan), not the whole Arab world. Just a short time ago, in a project as massive as NEOM, Saudi Arabia would have involved everyone.

The changing outlook of Saudi Arabia is leading to many new realities. First, a void is emerging as Saudi Arabia steps away from its traditional role. Who will lead the Arab world? And, in this void, unexpected leaders are likely to emerge. Except, these may not necessarily be nations, but also companies or even cities. Second, for decades, Saudi Arabia acted as a "gatekeeper" for the Middle East, controlling the footprint of foreign powers. Now, in the vertical world, the region may have no gatekeeper, allowing foreign powers to dominate the Middle East in new ways (or be thrown out completely).

But, what is the most significant change is this. For so long, there has been a desire to unify the Middle East. And, with globalization, there was a moment when this was possible. Now, however, the winds are moving in a different direction. The choices that nations are making with technology reflect a silent yet growing consensus that unifying the Middle East is no longer needed. With technology, governments are succeeding on their own.

And, this means that increasingly, the nations of the Middle East will look at the vertical world as a zero-sum game. There is no space for collaboration or cooperation. Everything is on the table. The winner takes everything. And the loser does not take the crumbs. The loser becomes the crumbs.

CHAPTER THREE

India Fights Against Next Colonialism

In the world's largest democracy, in the hearts and minds of 1.4 billion people, sovereignty holds a place like nothing else. The ability of India to decide its fate, to be free of foreign control, cuts across all lines, from religion to caste to age to socioeconomic status to geography. On every other issue, these factors divide India. But, on matters of sovereignty, India stands united. Any attack on India's sovereignty evokes feelings so strong that even minor border flare-ups threaten nuclear war.

Except, unlike much of the world, India's fight for sovereignty has not just been about territory but also globalization. Since independence, from free trade to foreign businesses, India has taken a cautious approach to how it opened up to the rest of the world. India did not want to become "occupied" or "controlled" again. However, while India may have been slow to adopt the global norms out of caution, it was still moving toward becoming more globalized. The barriers that separated India from the rest of the world were being brought down.

This strategy of becoming globalized is now being ripped apart when it comes to technology. For India, the spread of technology, enabled by barriers being knocked down (globalization), represents a threat. The government in New Delhi is concerned that as India allows in foreign technology, the shackles of colonialism will return. And that through technology, foreign powers could once again end up controlling India. Just like territory, India has begun to view technology as a challenge to its sovereignty. Now, India is rapidly entering the vertical world. It is bending technology to its will. It is establishing new barriers that control how technology can operate within the nation. And, India is leading a new paradigm where technology and nationalism coexist.

For India, the wounds of colonialism remain fresh. And, the fears of the past returning in a new form remain high. Forming the vertical world allows India to continue developing but hold the world at arm's length. But, what is taking place in India goes beyond this. As technology creates fears that India is losing sovereignty, the government is championing India in a new way. And, in the process, India may influence the whole world to exit globalization and act vertically.

Making Technology Firms "India First"

In India, technology companies are struggling to deal with the Indian government. Many companies are no longer deciding what to sell or how to operate. The Indian government is forcing these companies to prioritize India's sovereignty over their success. Operating like this goes against the model that technology firms have followed in the globalized world. Technology firms have been able to "transcend" borders and ignore local governments. They were able to take their services and products directly to consumers. Except, in India, this was not possible. The government has been acting vertically by establishing walls around technology. In India, technology firms are not driving globalization like they once were. They are not connecting India, or the Indian consumer, with the world. Instead, the government in New Delhi is using these firms to limit India's integration with the rest of the world.

To achieve this, India is using multiple strategies. One of them is to outright ban certain services. Take Facebook. For years, Facebook used globalization to expand across the world successfully. It faced little resistance (or ignored it). In India, Facebook expected to replicate this success. And, in India, Facebook had bigger ambitions than just offer its social media services. It had developed a service called "Facebook Basics." This was a basket of services that would be given to people in India for free to connect them to the Internet. However, with "Facebook Basics," Facebook would be deciding what services people in India had access to. This meant, for hundreds of millions of Indians, who would have been users of Facebook Basics, Facebook would have become the gatekeeper. A foreign firm would have been in charge of the Internet for people in India.

From the standpoint of globalization, this was acceptable, even normal. Through Facebook Basics, India would be integrating deeper into the world, and Indians would be using the same services everyone else was using. But, India did not see it this way. For India, Facebook Basics represented a form of "technology colonization," whereby a foreign power would control India's people in a new way. Ultimately, even after months of Facebook lobbying the Indian government, in February 2016, India banned Facebook Basics. [50] It was a message to the rest of the world that India was not playing games when it came to technology. It was willing to reject deeper integration with the world and take on the most prominent companies to protect the nation.

While India decided to ban Facebook Basics, it has taken a different approach with Amazon. Over the past several years, as e-commerce has taken off in India, the government has become concerned that Indian retailers and consumers are becoming hostage to e-commerce platforms like Amazon. If Amazon was an Indian company, the government might be concerned for different reasons (i.e., local brick and mortar stores going out of business because of digital vendors). But, because Amazon is a foreign company, the government is approaching e-commerce through the lens of sovereignty. To break the hold that firms like Amazon have, India has been making e-commerce vertical. In March 2016, India unveiled new laws for e-commerce companies that made it difficult for firms like Amazon to sell their own house brands. It did not want Amazon to sell its own brand of bedsheets and become a bedsheet monopoly.[51] In December 2018, India added new rules to its e-commerce laws, this time targeting suppliers. The new laws made it illegal for suppliers to accumulate more than 25% of their gross sales through a single e-commerce platform.[52] If a brand generated US$100 in gross sales, only US$25 could come from a single e-commerce platform. If a brand made US$30 from Amazon, under India's law, this would be illegal. India did not want its companies to become wholly dependent on foreign e-commerce platforms for their success. In India, Amazon has been forced to play a role it never imagined. Instead of prioritizing its own success, Amazon has been forced to prioritize India's sovereignty. And as a result, Amazon's business in India has been hit. Once the new e-commerce laws went into effect in February 2019, around 400,000 products, representing one-third of its US$6 billion sales in India, were up in the air.[53] Today, in India, Amazon is no longer connecting Indian consumers with international products. Instead, Amazon has become a new kind of middle man, connecting Indian consumers exclusively with Indian goods.

Like many other companies, firms like Facebook and Amazon entered India because of the massive, untapped opportunity. With more than 600 million people under the age of 25[54] and a middle class expected to balloon to 1 billion people by 2030[55], India represents a market like no other. And, with more than 400 million people on smartphones[56], India is morphing into a mobile-first economy, another boost for technology companies. And, while foreign companies have struggled with gaining proper access to the Indian market before, eventually, these challenges were solved. For example, today, Walmart is an established brand in India, with dozens of stores. But, this was not always the case. For years, Walmart's presence in India was limited to being a retailer for local goods sourced from Indian businesses. The foreign business laws in India were so strong that Walmart could not even open a store without giving some control to a local Indian partner. These challenges that foreign firms faced were a sign that India was still slow to buy into globalization. By controlling how foreign businesses could operate, India was maintaining its sovereignty. However, over time, India's laws changed as the economy opened up. And, in February 2020, after India changed some of its retail laws, Apple announced it would open its first retail store in India in 2021.[57]

Companies like Facebook and Amazon likely expected a similar situation to take place when they entered India. But, little did they know the vertical world was emerging in India. And that by acting vertically, India would turn their businesses upside down. While these firms were looking to India to succeed, India was looking to them to succeed in another way: limiting globalization.

Is the vertical world the new doctrine for India as it marches towards superpower status? The way India has been approaching technology companies is turning these firms into a kind of trade barrier. Certain services and goods can no longer enter India without facing hurdles and requirements. If companies do not comply, they will be banned. But, there is a caveat. As the world lines up to take advantage of India's rapid economic growth, nations may "ignore" India's vertical decisions. Whatever India does, from banning certain services to clamping down on specific platforms, the world might overlook because the Indian market is too big of an opportunity to lose out on. And this means that India could continue to build technology-based walls and barriers and still trade with the whole world - challenging the idea that globalization is the only path to develop and grow.

India Builds Borders Around Data And Drones

One part of the vertical world is about stopping technology from entering a nation (i.e., India not wanting Amazon to sell foreign goods). But, another part has to do with stopping technology, or what enables technology, from leaving a nation. Take data. For many decades, data moved freely around the world. Besides Russia, China, Iran, or North Korea, who were actively involved in controlling data, most governments did not come in the way of how data was collected, moved, or used. In recent years, the privacy and surveillance concerns, along with fears of technology firms becoming monopolies, have pushed governments to reassess their approach to data. For India, however, its data strategy has little to do with the traditional concerns and more to do with ensuring Indian companies remain in control of India's economy. Because technology firms are becoming the most powerful companies, India has begun transferring control of the ultimate resource (data) from foreign hands to Indian hands.

India's actions on data are taking place at multiple levels. First, for several years, India has been forcing data collected in India to be stored within India. Storing data this way is known as "data localization." In October 2018, the Reserve Bank of India (RBI) announced that financial companies, like Visa and MasterCard, would have to start storing data in India.[58] In December 2019, India unveiled a more holistic data framework, proposing data localization for every business in every sector.[59] The data localization push by India is not to be taken lightly. In April 2021, India banned American Express and Diners Club from adding new customers because they breached the data localization rules.[60] It was the first time India had punished a business over data localization. It meant that not complying with data rules could derail business operations in India.

Second, as India forces data to be stored locally, it is not allowing this data to sit on servers controlled by foreign companies. Instead, it is setting up a way for this data to be shared with Indian firms. In March 2018, Niti Aayog, the Indian government's think tank, announced it was developing a national strategy for AI. A big part of this strategy has to do with data.[61] More than a year later, in May 2019, Niti Aayog revealed that it was working to end the data monopolies held by large technology companies. It was looking to create an open marketplace for data.[62] And, shortly after this, in July 2019, Niti Aayog started asking for proposals to build this marketplace, known as the "National Data and Analytics Platform."[63]

Third, India is going beyond just data. To give Indian firms the "ultimate edge," India is targeting what data enables: AI. In July 2020, India unveiled new legislation that, if passed, would require Internet companies to hand over the source code, including algorithms, to the Indian government for inspection.[64]

India is taking a radical stance towards data. As India takes these steps, it is attacking globalization from multiple angles. India is acting externally at one angle, erecting new barriers to stop data from leaving the nation. And, at another angle, India is working internally, forcing technology firms to hand over their domestic edge to local companies. And, alongside all this, India is punishing foreign companies who do not align with its data rules. When it comes to data, India is going full vertical. Instead of technology removing borders, in India, technology is establishing new kinds of borders: data borders.

Of course, other nations are not happy with what India is doing. One of these nations is the US. In June 2019, following India's stance on localizing data, the US threatened to limit how many H1B visas are handed to Indian high-skilled immigrants if the data policies were not changed.[65] For the first time, data rules threatened to influence immigration. At one moment, technology firms are losing their edge in India because of data localization. At another moment, because of data, those same technology firms may face disruptions at home (in the US) over visas not being handed out to Indian talent.

A similar push is underway in India with drones. With drones, India does not want to become reliant on other nations. But, instead of outright banning drones imported from abroad, India is establishing a new system that may naturally "phase out" foreign drones in the coming years. In August 2020, India launched "Digital Sky." This is a platform to manage drone traffic. Through it, more than 70% of India's territory is drone-friendly. [66] Tucked away in the rules is a section governing foreign drones, like those from DJI (China) or Parrot (France). If these drone companies do not comply with Digital Sky, their products will be banned in India. And most of the foreign drones do not comply. Why? Because Digital Sky requires drones to be manufactured with specific requirements. One of these requirements is that they can receive a certain kind of "firmware update." And, foreign drone firms, like DJI, have refused to offer this.[67]

While India establishes explicit borders around data, with drones, India is erecting implicit borders. The government does not want India's society to be dominated by a flood of foreign technology, like consumer drones. If this were to occur, local Indian drone companies would be outcompeted, allowing foreign companies - and nations - to dominate a critical industry. The influx of foreign drones also raises national security challenges, such as those around drone surveillance and drone terrorism. Through Digital Sky, India is tackling all these issues at once. And, in the process, a new barrier is being built that limits how an entire technology can be bought, sold, and deployed in India. With drones, India is "blocking out" the whole world from its consumers and territory. And, by making this decision, India might cause companies who cannot access the Indian market to become less valuable. Can a drone company from the US or Japan get funding if they cannot access one of the world's largest markets?

Alongside all this, while India takes steps to limit foreign consumer drones, it is doubling down on military drones from the US and Israel. Again, the vertical paradox returns as India moves on two fronts simultaneously, pushing out foreign consumer drones and allowing foreign military drones in.

At the center of many of these moves, alongside sovereignty, is self-sufficiency. The next design of India's society and economy may rely on technologies like drones (i.e., drone delivery for logistics). India does not want to fall into a trap where another nation can control it by stopping certain exports or using drone data to give themselves a competitive edge. Instead of abiding by the established global norms, which allow drones to be sold worldwide, India is charting its own path. The new industries, like drones, are being looked at through a vertical lens.

Splitting From China On The Back Of Nationalism

Driven by nationalism, India is overhauling its relationship with China. But, to do this, India is turning to technology. In India, nationalism and technology are feeding off each other. While India has been suspicious of China for decades, the impetus for India to "unplug" from Chinese technology was the border flare-up in the Himalayas in June 2020. As both sides moved tens of thousands of soldiers into the area, ratcheting up tensions even more, the most immediate way India responded was through technology. Shortly after the flare-up, India's intelligence agencies issued a security alert for 52 apps with links to the Chinese government.[68] And, just a week after this, India banned 59 Chinese apps, including TikTok and WeChat, which were previously flagged.[69] In August 2020, India's government prepared to unveil rules that would effectively ban Chinese firms, like Huawei and ZTE, from building India's 5G network.[70] And, in September 2020, India banned a further 118

Chinese apps, including the popular game "PlayerUnknown's Battlegrounds (PUBG)."[71] While the Indian and Chinese soldiers stared eyeball-to-eyeball at each other in the Himalayas, the war had already begun in the technology realm.

As India takes these steps, some Chinese firms are realizing that India is becoming "off-limits." In August 2020, Alibaba said it would be halting investments in India for at least six months amidst souring relations.[72] And, in the same month, the Chinese smartphone maker "Vivo" said it would not be sponsoring the "Indian Premier League (IPL)," the most significant sports event in India.[73] But then, in February 2021, Vivo returned as the sponsor.[74] In April 2021, India took fresh action against ByteDance, the parent company of TikTok, freezing its local Indian bank account over "tax evasion." The court said it would unfreeze the account once ByteDance deposited US$11 million.[75] And, starting in November 2020, India has been blocking the imports of Chinese electronics that contain Wi-Fi hardware, creating headaches for the likes of Xiaomi, Oppo, and Dell.[76]

Of course, the sword cuts both ways. As Chinese technology firms leave India or halt investments, it is affecting India's startup scene. Those working in India's technology sector are being forced to look for new job opportunities.[77] Except, it is not just Chinese or Indian firms that are being affected. Alongside Dell (and HP) being affected by India blocking Chinese electronic imports, in June 2020, India announced new laws that would force e-commerce companies like Amazon to show how much of a product was manufactured in India.[78] This means, when an Indian consumer is shopping for plastic containers, they would see that 20% of the product was "Made in India." Alternatively, they might see that 100% of the product was Made in China. In a subtle way, India is "activating" citizens with this law, making them think patriotically when purchasing goods. And, with this new law, suddenly, Amazon is morphing into a tool of the Indian government to fight another nation. The Amazon e-commerce platform has suddenly become "weaponized" by India to control how two of the largest economies in the Indo-Pacific do business. By forcing Amazon to label items based on country of origin, India has established a new cultural barrier using technology.

What India is doing to Chinese technology represents a new reality.

In the old model of globalization, it would take decades for nations like India and China to disconnect from each other fully. In fact, complete disconnection may have been impossible. But, in the vertical world, when it comes to technology, the disconnection is taking place in a matter of weeks and months. The integration between two nations, built on the back of globalization, could be destroyed, because of technology, at a pace few think is possible.

Conclusion

Just like in the 20th century, India is fighting for independence again. Unlike in the past, when India was a colony retaliating against an empire, today, India is fighting for freedom "preemptively." It knows that unless it is careful, technology will lead to a new kind of colonialism. And, it must take action now before it is too late. At the center of this is globalization. The more India buys into globalization, reducing barriers, opening up industries, or adopting global platforms, the more technology will spread in India unfettered. And, the more India will be at risk. This means, to stop the threat that technology poses, India has to stop globalization.

For India, the vertical world is not a choice. It is a necessity to protect sovereignty and remain independent. But, India is entering the vertical world at an unusual time. Unlike the US, which is the global leader, or China, which has rapidly developed, India is still rising and developing. In other words, the US and China used globalization to grow and build their global footprint. But, India is already jumping ship without even achieving the same status.

As India does this, it is pioneering a new model for the world. For years, India has been a "poster child" for other nations who wanted to emerge out of the shadows of colonialism and develop on their own. The decisions that India took in the past, from signing trade deals to partnering on climate change, were seen as "wins" by the established order. India was buying into globalization and becoming a "stakeholder." But, now, when it comes to technology, India is going in the opposite direction. If India succeeds, even as it establishes new barriers, it will create a problem for other nations who seek to rise up. Should they buy into the globalized model or the vertical model?

Many years ago, those who analyzed India's growth saw a nation that was becoming globalized. To prove this, analysis would show that young people were wearing iconic logos and following popular culture. Or that urban centers were being built for global brands. All expectations were that India's adoption of globalization would only grow. The only question was how India would balance its modern aspirations with its ancient roots. This was the narrow keyhole India was looked at through. And, it left out an important question: while globalization wanted India, would India always want (or desire) globalization? With the actions India is taking on technology, the world has its answer.

CHAPTER FOUR

Raising The Korean Flag

After the Korean War in 1953, South Korea was in a state of paranoia. The Korean peninsula was unstable. And, while South Korea had become independent, it was surrounded on all sides by nations who had either fought against it or enslaved it. Without taking bold steps, South Korea knew it would be living under the shadow of countries it did not trust. And it would become reliant on these same nations for its livelihood. This fate was not an option. And, so, at a time when the world was just waking up to globalization, South Korea went full steam ahead. It started adopting all kinds of global ideas, in part, to ensure it remained free.

Except, South Korea was not able to do this alone. To rise with globalization, it needed assistance. And, this assistance came in the form of the US offering military protection and access to the US market. The deeper the US-South Korea relationship became, the more "globalized" South Korea became. At first, globalization for South Korea was all about the economy. It started by establishing itself as a manufacturing hub. Then, it built global brands in the automotive, electronics, and appliance industries. And, in more recent years, South Korea turned into a global technology powerhouse. Then, over time, globalization started to influence other parts of South Korea too. South Korea brought baseball into Korean society. On foreign policy, it developed a strong relationship with Japan to keep America happy. Within a short period, for South Korea, globalization and Americanization became the same thing.

However, even as this took place and South Korea rapidly developed, the government in Seoul was always uneasy with the status quo. This meant it was never comfortable with being reliant on another nation - the US. But, for so long, South Korea had no choice except to remain pegged to the US model. The only path to success was globalization.

Fast forward to today. A new thinking has begun in South Korea as it uses technology to create new sovereignty for itself. The gradual steps that South Korea is taking are creating "cracks" in the model it has followed for decades.

With technology, South Korea is unplugging from globalization and entering the vertical world. It is drawing lines between itself and the rest of the world, especially the US. The way South Korea has operated for decades is rapidly changing. Just as globalization designed South Korea a certain way, the vertical world is redesigning South Korea from the inside out.

Technology Taxes Reinforce South Korea's Borders

Most nations use taxes to raise revenue. South Korea, however, has a different strategy. The government in Seoul is using taxes on technology as barriers to "control" how businesses operate. In August 2017, South Korea approved the world's first "robot tax." The new policy restricts the amount of tax incentives given to firms investing in certain types of robots, like those replacing humans in the workplace.[79] By limiting tax incentives, South Korea is forcing companies in a particular direction: use humans over robots. Through this action, South Korea is entering the vertical world. A key tenet of globalization is that labor is accessible anywhere in the world, with little or no barriers. This means that companies can hire labor from any part of the world. An apparel company in the US can tap labor in Bangladesh, or a British tea brand can acquire labor in Kenya. However, the robot tax in South Korea turns this paradigm on its head.

The new labor forces, like those made up of robots, are being de-incentivized through regulation. Through the robot tax, South Korea is creating an indirect wall between businesses and robot labor. These new labor forces cannot be accessed freely like human labor forces can. Unlike in the globalized world, when human labor has been accessible to anyone, new labor forces have barriers, like taxes, around them in the vertical world. The tax is a new technology-based barrier to help humans stay in jobs. This also means that, through a robot tax, South Korea is creating a double standard. When it comes to the human labor force, South Korea has allowed the whole world in, with minor restrictions. But, when it comes to a robot labor force, South Korea is using public policy to create new walls. The same issue (labor) is being approached differently in the vertical world compared to the globalized world.

Another area where South Korea is using taxes to create the vertical world is digital currencies. In January 2020, the Korean government proposed a 20% tax on the trading of cryptocurrencies.[80] Of course, trading in any form is taxed. But, what makes this step different is that South Korea has been actively regulating the cryptocurrency space to stop it. In January 2018, the government unveiled new regulations that banned anonymous trading of cryptocurrencies and made it illegal for foreigners to engage in the activity.[81] And, in January 2020, South Korea unveiled another raft of rules, many of which intended to help the government crackdown on money laundering through cryptocurrencies.[82] The government in Seoul appears to be making it difficult for people to use/trade digital currencies.

While South Korea is clamping down on cryptocurrencies, it is preparing its own "central bank digital currency," or CBDC. In October 2020, the Bank of Korea announced it would begin trials of the CBDC ending in December 2021. The trials would examine how to deploy the digital currency throughout Korean society.[83] Like with the robot tax, South Korea is quietly pushing its society in a particular direction with its digital currency. It does not want any form of digital currency to dominate, including those from other nations. It wants its own CBDC to become the main form of payment. At one level, countries using their currency within their borders is nothing new. But, for South Korea, a nation that has not challenged globalization because there was no other way, the CBDC may give rise to new thinking.

For example, South Korea could start settling trade with its own CBDC, no longer using USD or Euro for critical transactions like those around energy. But, it also means that South Korea could start to force its currency in markets overseas. Take a look at self-driving cars. As self-driving vehicles become mobile shopping centers, Korean automotive companies like Hyundai or Kia could introduce Digital Won inside the shopping centers operating in their self-driving cars. If people wanted to shop, they would have no choice but to use the South Korean digital currency.

Similarly, the Korean appliance industry, which is increasingly making "connected products," may integrate Digital Won. An intelligent fridge monitoring what groceries are running low may initiate a purchase from a local store in Digital Won. This would not be the first time South Korea has taken a direct role in promoting a sovereign interest. In 2009, to boost South Korea's global reputation in food production, Seoul established "The Kimchi Institute." [84] This institute started to analyze markets, like the US and Japan, and altered Kimchi for different taste buds. Then, the Korean government supported the creation of Korean restaurants in those destinations. Spreading local food around the world has come to be known as "gastro-diplomacy."

There is another way South Korea can make its digital currency acceptable if the government cannot take Digital Won to the world. It can force the world to adopt the money if it wants to do business in South Korea. For instance, foreigners entering the country may be forced to hold a certain amount of Digital Won as a "precondition" for receiving an entry visa. Such an action would result in South Korea pushing global currencies aside and building a vertical wall with Digital Won.

The South Korean government is also using penalties (fines) on foreign technology firms to create the vertical world. In December 2016, South Korea's antitrust regulator issued an US$853 million fine against Qualcomm.[85] The reason for the fine - the highest ever imposed on a company in South Korea - was two-part. First, Qualcomm was charging royalties that South Korea viewed as unfair. Second, and more importantly, Qualcomm was refusing to share its chip patents with local Korean competitors like Samsung.[86] By taking this step against Qualcomm, South Korea reasserted its borders in a new way. The fine meant that technology firms like Qualcomm could no longer operate in South Korea without any limits. Now, foreign technology firms would have to support the local Korean ecosystem or face massive penalties. In many ways, the fine against Qualcomm was a message to the world that to operate in South Korea, technology firms cannot ignore the Korean aspirations.

This is a new, vertical dynamic for South Korea. For decades, different governments in Seoul adopted globalization to develop the country and define its place globally. Now, a new and different attitude is emerging. South Korea is using taxes and fines as a way to change its presence in the world. There is also another way to look at this. South Korea wants to dominate foreign markets, but it does not want to be dominated by foreign nations.

Post-Covid Korea Looks At The World Differently

The Covid-19 pandemic put every nation in a corner. As the traditional economic drivers, like manufacturing and retail, slowed down, the old economic plans and paradigms lost steam. And, as economies came to a standstill, tens of millions of people lost jobs, prompting governments to introduce massive stimulus to keep their societies functioning. This was a wake-up call for governments. They had to create a new economic strategy and do it fast, or their nations would fall apart. Amidst massive uncertainty over when the pandemic would end (and when a vaccine would arrive), some governments were quick to announce new economic plans.

One of those nations was South Korea. In May 2020, South Korea unveiled the "New Deal" to grow the economy after the pandemic.[87] At the core of it was AI and 5G. Seoul is betting on these technologies to become the new driving forces. Except, as this strategy is implemented, it could allow South Korea to become less reliant on the world. For example, in November 2018, the South Korean government passed a new law allowing "AI Employment."[88] The law permitted South Korean pharmaceutical companies to use AI for research and development (like designing medicines). This means, instead of hiring foreign talent to come to South Korea to work or open up labs in foreign markets, the South Korean pharmaceutical companies instead could "hire" algorithms developed locally.

In other words, AI could enable nations to reduce their dependency on the rest of the world by supplying capabilities that were once imported. It may allow governments to act vertically. And, as this happens, South Korea is likely to question how much it needs globalization in the first place.

South Korea is also taking action to acquire next-generation talent locally. In August 2020, the South Korean city of Daegu, located in the southern part of

Korea, announced it was putting aside US$6 million to train people in AI and blockchain. Could South Korea develop the talent it needs at home instead of sending its people abroad or bringing people from abroad? For a long time, nations have sent their best abroad to a handful of schools to "train them up." Except, now, when it comes to emerging fields, like blockchain, nations are building human capital domestically. They are reducing their reliance on the world for talent, skills, or education. A significant "connection" that countries have had with the rest of the world - sending people abroad for education - is being severed with emerging technologies. One of the reasons nations are turning inward (i.e., acting vertically) when it comes to next-generation talent is because experts are hard to come by. Unlike in traditional fields, like business or economics, where there have been a handful of "experts" in the world, there are no one set of experts or schools when it comes to areas like AI and blockchain. This means nations are able to not only train talent at home but keep this talent at home too. Of course, this does not mean immigration will stop. But, it may mean that South Korea looks at immigration through a more "vertical" lens.

Quite surprisingly, even before the pandemic, South Korea was thinking vertically. In October 2015, the government handed Samsung a contract for US$14.8 million to develop robots that can replace Chinese labor. While the whole world was busy outsourcing their supply chains to China, alarm bells were already ringing in South Korea that relying on other economies too much was a significant risk. Instead of Korean firms using Chinese factories, South Korea wanted Korean firms to use Korean robots in Korean factories.[89]

The push to unplug from China represents another paradox in the vertical world. On the one hand, South Korea is trying to de-incentivize businesses from using robot labor with a robot tax. But, on the other hand, with Samsung's contract, South Korea is incentivizing companies to use robot labor. And, both of these counter moves are driving the vertical world. At one moment, South Korea is building walls to limit robot labor (i.e., robot tax). And, at another moment, South Korea is using robot labor to limit economic integration (i.e., bringing manufacturing back home). Under globalization, everybody moves in the same direction (i.e., fewer barriers, more open markets). But, in the vertical world, governments can make one decision and then act 180 degrees differently on the same related decision. These choices do not cancel each other out. They drive and complement each other in the vertical world since these choices are both aimed at limiting dependence on the global community.

Walking Away From The US World Order

It is not wrong to say that whatever South Korea is today, it is in part because of its close relationship with the US. However, today, this relationship could be in jeopardy because of South Korea's vertical steps with technology. In August 2011, South Korea announced it would be supporting a local open-source mobile operating system (OS) to replace Android and iOS. This was surprising. Because, when it came to defense or culture, South Korea was deeply plugged into the American way. But, when it came to mobile OS, South Korea was trying to unplug from the US. To build a local OS, the Korean government would bring together large firms like LG and Samsung. The goal was to have the local OS loaded on all Korean mobile devices.[90] In January 2015, Samsung launched a new smartphone called "Z1." The US$92 phone was developed for consumers in markets like India. And it did not use Android. It used Samsung's OS called "Tizen." This represented the beginning of an independent OS emerging in South Korea. Today, Tizen powers Samsung's entire lineup of wearables.[91]

Why is one of America's closest allies building its own OS? Part of it has to do with commercial realities. South Korea does not want its most important companies sourcing software from a competitor (i.e., Samsung using Google's Android while Google builds phones that compete with Samsung). But, another reason may be that Seoul senses that this is a "way out" of the established, US-led model. South Korea may feel that it has reached a point where it can start taking steps it could not take before, including reducing its dependency on the US. Instead of standing on the US-built foundation, South Korea may want to create its own foundation going into the future. And, this means that systems that were once imported, like an OS, will now be developed locally.

The global reach of software, which has connected the world like never before, is now facing limits as nations like South Korea move in a different direction. The new Korean OS may act as a new technology wall. Once South Korea has its own OS, will it still allow Android or iOS in the country? Or, just like with a robot tax, could South Korea introduce an "OS tax" that seeks to restrict foreign software, which is predominantly American?

While South Korea builds its own OS, it is also splitting from the US in another area: containing Chinese technology. In October 2020, as the US lobbied countless nations to ban Huawei's 5G technology, South Korea took a different stance. In a meeting with US diplomats, a South Korean official said the decision on Huawei lies with the private sector, not the government.[92] In other words, Seoul would not ban Huawei and was leaving it up to its businesses to decide what to do. Months before this, as the US targeted Chinese technology firms, South Korea continued to allow many Chinese firms to operate in sensitive areas. In May 2020, Huawei launched a 5G lab in Seoul. But, on purpose, Huawei did not make a loud noise about it. It had just been blacklisted by the US.[93] In June 2020, Huawei announced a deal with South Korea to help Korean AI startups expand globally.[94] And, in the same month, amidst US chip restrictions on Huawei, Samsung said it was looking into supplying chips to the Chinese firm irrespective.[95] These steps are a sign that technology is causing the US-South Korea relationship to crack. Unlike with OS, where the "split" is less visible, the divergence on Chinese technology is public. And, unlike in the past, when Seoul resoundingly supported US decisions, now, through technology, a different reality is emerging. South Korea is using technology to break away from its most important ally and make its own decisions on world affairs.

Conclusion

The design of South Korea is undergoing a massive change. South Korea's foundation for decades is now morphing into something new, unfamiliar, and vertical. Instead of remaining reliant on the US and other parts of the world, South Korea is building a new kind of independence for itself with technology. Of course, what is taking place right now are just baby steps. But, quite rapidly, what South Korea is doing could become something much bigger.

At one level, a vertical South Korea will create a new design for the Indo-Pacific. South Korea's decisions will allow the government in Seoul to play a more significant role in the region, one that other powers might view as a threat or infringement. However, at another level, the more South Korea acts vertically, the more it will affect the US footprint in the world. For decades, the US has built its influence, in part, by bringing nations like South Korea into its orbit. But, this "strength" is also a weakness. If those nations leave the US orbit, then the US loses power.

Of course, there are many unknowns when it comes to South Korea's march into the vertical world. For example, what will a vertical South Korea mean for North Korea? Or, how will the world's technology supply chains operate if South Korea is building new walls? Except, the biggest unknown is what the "new" culture of South Korea will be. For a long time, South Korea has been "pegged" to other nations, either directly controlled by them or living under their shadows. Now, the vertical world presents a new opportunity for South Korea to truly become independent in a way that has not been possible in recent times. This is far bigger than just a redesigning of the economy or business landscape. Acquiring a new kind of sovereignty can lead to a new culture and attitude within a nation.

The next South Korea, a direct outcome of the vertical world, will look very different from what exists today. The so-called "Asian Tiger," a phrase given to

South Korea in the 20th century, may return. Except, this time, it may be used to describe a nation that is acting aggressively to carve out a place on the world stage in a way that disrupts everyone else. And forces nations, including those who were once close allies, to either move over or fight back.

CHAPTER FIVE

A Walled Off Russia

When the Soviet Union dissolved, Russia was in an awkward place. All of a sudden, the Cold War was over. All of the planning and thinking for "grand competition" with the US got pushed aside. The government in Moscow was focused on keeping the Russian economy functioning and society afloat. There was little discussion as to what was Russia's role in the post-Soviet Union world. The next decades for Russia revolved around two areas: energy and defense. By developing massive energy reserves, Russia dominated the natural gas and oil markets. And, through steady military modernization, Russia rebuilt its capabilities in the world.

Except, as all of this happened, Russia found itself tied to a model that was increasingly becoming uncomfortable. The model began to suffocate Russia and its people. It was not that Russia did not like globalization. It was that Russia did not like globalization in its current form. It did not want to play by rules set by the US or the West. Russia felt that the way the world was structured was causing it to lose power over itself. And that it could not take advantage of opportunities that globalization potentially offered.

To fight back, Russia used several strategies. First, it played the waiting game, hoping that as nations like India and China developed, they too would challenge globalization. Russia was looking forward to the day when a group of countries would stand together against the prevailing system of globalization. Second, Russia quietly developed its own technology leadership, investing in areas that most Western analyses did not catch (or care about). For instance, while the world watched the US, Israel, or China for AI, Russia also built itself into an AI leader. In June 2020, Russia trialed AI that allowed soldiers to give robots orders verbally (through voice).[96] Third, Russia realized that it could "lead" without the Soviet Union. And that there were strategic opportunities to challenge the established order (i.e., taking action in Syria).

Those strategies - of strategic patience, new technological capabilities, and independent action - have converged, with technology as the foundation. And, the convergence is leading to new futures. At one level, Russia is challenging globalization by offering nations technology that allows them to act vertically. But, at another level, Russia is taking a more radical stance. In some cases, it is "blocking out" the world through technology like the Internet. Instead of using the Internet to integrate deeper into the world, Russia is using it to walk away from the world. The government in Moscow has realized that with technology, it has new "tools." And, with these tools, it does not need to operate the way it once did. And it does not necessarily need other nations for support. With technology, Russia can take steps it could not take before and regain control it believes it has lost.

Russia Unplugs From The Global Internet

In the 21st century, the Internet has been one of the biggest drivers of globalization. As of October 2020, there were 4.66 billion people on the Internet, representing 59% of the world's population. People no longer have to cross oceans to communicate, form relationships or conduct business. Through the Internet, everything from finance to e-commerce to education is possible. Traditionally, through the lens of globalization, the Internet has been a way to scale economies. The more people go online, the more societies are connected, the more it will result in commerce and economic activity. Except, now, there is a different lens to view the Internet through. The vertical lens. The new lens gives nations the ability to build barriers and separate themselves from the world and then build a new strategy for integrating with the world on their terms.

Besides China, the nation leading this vertical paradigm for the Internet is Russia. In February 2019, the Russian government proposed the "Digital Economy National Program." This is a program to build a "domestic Internet." The Russian government was worried that geopolitics could cause the Internet to become weaponized. To counter this, Moscow wanted a domestic network that would allow Internet activity within Russia to depend on local servers and systems - instead of ones located abroad.[97] In December 2019, Russia said it had successfully fired up its domestic Internet but did not reveal many details except that Internet users in Russia would not have seen any changes.[98] Instead of using the Internet to build deeper inroads with the world, Russia is taking a different approach. It is developing a domestic version of the Internet that is "independent" of what exists globally.

A domestic Internet is a two-prong attack on globalization. First, Russia can block out the world with its domestic Internet. And, second, Russia is "exiting" the systems, like the global Internet, that the rest of the world uses. Some may call Russia's domestic Internet a new kind of "intranet," the domestic networks that have existed in companies (and cities) for decades. Except, this is not accurate. Intranets, in all their forms, have complemented the global Internet. They have never replaced it. An employee in a multinational uses the company intranet for their work activity. But, once they leave the office, they are back on the worldwide web that everyone else is using. In other words, the Internet has never been a case of "one or the other." In Russia, however, the "two Internets" could soon be the new reality.

At one level, this means that unlike in the past, when a single Internet governed the world, soon, there may be multiple "Internets" operating and originating from different parts of the world. Instead of everyone plugged into the same global system (i.e., the world wide web), nations will be plugged into other, opposing systems. This makes the new Internets "walls" that separate people and nations from one another. It is the complete opposite of globalization. This will divide the world in a new way and represent a further barrier to business. From financial services to mobile apps, every company will have to rethink how to operate in an era of domestic or country-specific Internets. That is because nations with this Internet setup, like Russia, will be able to restrict specific platforms and services in ways that many businesses do not expect or are used to. This means that startups or multinationals from new technology sectors, hoping to access the Russian market with little resistance, may face new and unfamiliar challenges coming from the Russian government. These firms might be slowed, suspended, or outright banned to ensure

Russian companies can stay competitive. A domestic Internet could represent a new way to block foreign companies and give local industries a boost.

What makes a domestic Internet so controversial is that the same variable driving globalization is now also driving the vertical world. The "two sides of globalization" are becoming more apparent. That is, at one moment, the Internet has been a force that reduced barriers, integrated societies, and connected people. Then, at the next moment, instead of lowering barriers, a domestic Internet is establishing them. Instead of integrating or connecting the world, new forms of the Internet are dividing it.

There is also the possibility that Russia selectively connects with other nations through its domestic Internet. One of these nations could be Iran. In August 2016, the Iranian government announced it had successfully tested its domestic Internet, or what it called a "National Internet." This has also been referred to as a "halal Internet."[99] For Iran, it wanted such an Internet to enhance Islamic teachings and improve the population's digital skills. Of course, a National Internet also serves another purpose: giving Iran's government more control over society.[100] For now, Iran is looking at its National

Internet through the domestic lens. But, in the near future, might Russia and Iran connect their "local" Internets? These Internet connections would represent new, exclusive corridors between nations that block out much of the world. Instead of governments using the established, global channels, they would be using domestic Internets to build one-on-one relations. On the back of this, domestic Internets can evolve into regional Internets that include other nations. In the case of Russia and Iran, countries like China, Afghanistan, and Pakistan could be invited to join. China may already be part of Iran's Internet strategy. In September 2020, as part of a 25-year agreement between Iran and China, a deal was struck for China to help build a National Internet in Iran.[101] All of this means, in the vertical world, a domestic Internet could serve as the foundation for entire regions to "unplug" from globalization and build their own regional "digital blocs."

The emergence of a domestic Internet in Russia matters for another reason: it puts the West on edge. The Internet has long been under the control of Western powers. And, Russia has been stuck with this model. The domestic Internet takes this control away and places it in the hands of the Russian government. It establishes

Russian sovereignty in a new way. However, in this process, Russia's domestic Internet could cause Russia to become more "isolated" than ever before.

A domestic Internet represents a new option for nations unhappy with the current global Internet setup. If Russia wants, within minutes, it will be able to disconnect itself from the worldwide Internet, restricting and redefining how the Russian society and economy integrate with the rest of the world. In the vertical world, the most radical steps, which were once unthinkable, are fast becoming a reality.

Automation To Replace Immigration In Russia

Like the Internet, the current design of the immigration systems around the world has also driven globalization. The movement of people, businesses, and ideas has integrated the world on a much deeper level. And, since many nations have had the same goal with immigration, that is, to attract people and businesses, it appeared for a long time that this global strategy of immigration was never going to change. But, now, as technology advances, a different thought process is emerging. Do nations still need immigrants in the age of robots? Could automation replace immigration? Such an idea was unthinkable just a few years ago. Now, going forward, if automation starts to replace immigration, one of the biggest drivers of globalization will be discarded in its current form. And, one of the first countries that could turn to this model is Russia.

Like Japan and Germany, Russia faces a major demographic challenge. By 2050, Russia's population is expected to decline from 145.9 million people in 2019 to 135.8 million, a reduction of 7%. [102] The common wisdom would suggest that increasing immigration is the way to reverse population decline. Unlike Japan or Germany, which are trying to boost population numbers through immigration, Russia appears to be focusing more on automation. This can be seen because Russia has not made any significant changes to its immigration policies in recent times. But, when it comes to technology, specifically automation, Russia is making big bets. For example, the largest bank in Russia, Sberbank, has been heavily deploying AI throughout its operations. In January 2017, Sberbank announced it would be replacing 3,000 personnel in its legal division with a "robot lawyer" - a type of AI software. A year before this, in September 2016, the bank's CEO said that by 2021, AI would be managing 80% of the bank's decisions.[103]

It is not just banks that are replacing workers with robots in Russia. The oil industry is also looking at similar measures. In October 2019, Russian media mentioned that oil workers in the country would be monitored by an AI system called "Cyclops." The system can monitor many variables, including worker safety and whether a worker has the authorization to be on a site.[104] This could represent the beginning of AI taking over one of Russia's most critical industries. And, it is not just the finance and energy sectors that are starting to use AI. The Russian armed forces are also rolling out automation. In April 2020, an official in the "Advanced Research Foundation," Russia's military research and development division, warned that military robots would soon replace human soldiers.[105]

Clearly, Russia is moving forward with robots much faster than importing talent from outside its borders. As Russia develops more advanced robots, it may start to approach immigration more vertically. Is this the new direction for Russia? The automation of jobs may only reinforce Russia's decision to replace immigration with automation. Suppose robots result in millions of jobs disappearing in Russia. In that case, the Russian government may be forced to double down on helping the existing population find work, not bring in new people. How big a problem could this be? A study found that 20 million people could lose jobs to robots by 2030, more than a third of the entire Russian labor force.[106]

Immigration has long integrated the world by allowing people to move to different locations. Now, technology is changing this. As governments question the need to bring people in the first place, technology will become a new barrier that restricts where people can move. It will also cause governments to question the need to bring people in the first place. In other words, in the vertical world, people will not just face new limits around where they can immigrate too. In nations like Russia, they may have to convince authorities whether they are more competitive than robots. This new approach may motivate other governments to question immigration too. And, in societies where there is rising nationalism and growing concern about the types of people being let into the country, the movement towards automation over immigration may be accelerated.

As robots upend immigration, a new, unfamiliar future could emerge: will robots become the next immigrants? Unlike with globalization, when it was the movement of people that defined nations, in the vertical world, it may be the movement of robots that defines nations, societies, cultures, and borders.

A New Wild West In Space

In January 1967, the United Nations (UN) put into force legislation to govern space.[107] It was called the "Outer Space Treaty." This treaty was, and still is to this day, the only formal space law in the world. It covers areas like how space can be explored or how the Moon can be used. At the time of signing, there were only three signatories: the US, the United Kingdom, and the Soviet Union (now the Russian Federation). When this treaty was created, the world was a different place. There were only two real space powers: the US and Soviet Union. And, this made creating and following rules easy. Through this treaty, there was a baseline for how nations should conduct themselves in space. And, equally important, there was mutual benefit if countries complied: they could explore space without scrutiny or suspicion.

Except, since then, the makeup of the world has changed. Space is no longer the domain of just the US and Russia. There is also India, China, Japan, France, Morocco, UAE, Nigeria, and Israel. Space has become more crowded. As a result, the rules created in 1967, which once guided nations in space, have become outdated. This is leading to space becoming like a new "Wild West." Governments are ignoring the Outer Space Treaty, ignoring each other and doing whatever they want. There is no institution to govern space. There are no rules or laws. Nations are moving in a direction where space will become divided and not remain open and accessible.

Like the US and China, Russia is also fueling this new Wild West status quo in space. In November 2019, Russia announced plans to build a base on the Moon in the 2020s. [108] This base, exclusively for Russia, will monitor space debris and asteroids and prepare space missions to other planets like Mars. Before this, in September 2019, Russia and China had announced new cooperation in space, including establishing a data center for lunar missions and deep space exploration.[109]

At the same time, a critical link between the US and Russian space programs ended in April 2020. For years, the US has relied on Russian rockets to launch space missions. In April, the US marked its last space mission using these rockets. Going forward, the US will use its technology and companies.[110] This is a divergence from the past when both the US and Russia needed each other to reach space. Now, as both sides cut this dependence, they may act more "independently" than ever before, refusing to follow the rules set by the other side.

There are also the indirect ways that Russia is driving the vertical world in space. In July 2019, Russia said it would share certain technologies with India to help New Delhi with a manned-spacecraft program called "Gaganyaan."[111] This program is part of India's efforts to have an Indian space station equal to the International Space Station (ISS). India does not want to be tied to the "global" model in space, like the ISS. It wants its own, independent presence. And, to help India achieve this and challenge the West, Russia is supplying technology. As Russia and India move in this direction, they are breaking the hold that a few nations have had over space affairs.

On top of all this, private space enterprises are emerging, helping Russia lay claim to space in new ways. In July 2019, StartRocket, a Russian startup, unveiled plans for giant ads in space. The startup envisions groups of satellites using mirrors to broadcast advertisements, like logos or corporate messages, in the night sky.[112] What that means is that wherever these satellites are, at that moment, that portion of space may be deemed "Russian." This is a new way for nations to expand their borders (and reinforce them). The Russian advertising satellites will allow Russia to share messages with the world, from company logos to government statements, without depending on the current global systems. Could Russia use "vertical space" to influence geopolitics on Earth? The advertising satellites also mean that, in the vertical world, industries like advertising, which never had to think about geopolitics, will now be held captive by it.

As Russia supports its own space companies, the government in Moscow is going after space companies from other nations. This is also creating new barriers in space. In August 2019, OneWeb, a British space Internet company, was banned from supplying Internet in Russia. The Russian government refused to give OneWeb a permit citing national security laws around Internet traffic.[113] Russia's decision against OneWeb means the borders of Earth are extending into space. Even though

Russia cannot claim a part of space for itself yet, it is still forcing companies in space to operate according to Russian law.

In other words, space-based Internet is incompatible with globalization. These companies are not able to access the whole world. They are being blocked out from different nations from the get-go. These companies are being forced to act vertically and beam Internet selectively, based on which governments approve them.

Of course, in the vertical world, technology companies have equal power to governments. This means the space Internet firms could flat out ignore government rulings and beam the Internet to the world. This makes technology companies new stakeholders, like countries and institutions. It means that technology firms could establish their own "corporate borders" based on where they supply services. And these corporate borders will clash with the boundaries of other nations. Governments will be forced to take radical action against technology companies to protect sovereignty. In the case of space Internet, could a nation attack satellites that are beaming down Internet illegally? In the vertical world, conflicts will not just be between countries but also countries and technology companies.

Conclusion

What is Russia's role in the world? This has not been clear since the end of the Soviet Union. During the 1990s, over just a few years, Russia was rapidly pushed into the existing global structures dominated by the US. And, at the same time, Russia became dependent on "traditional" variables of geopolitics like energy and defense to build its economy and global footprint. This made Russia both a benefactor and a victim of globalization. However, now, after decades, the government in Moscow is creating some distance between itself and the rest of the globalized world through technology. Russia can erect new technology-based barriers limiting how much of a "say" the rest of the world has in Russia (i.e., the domestic Internet). Or how much "control" the established powers have over the rest of the world (i.e., helping India build its independent presence in space).

At the same time, Russia has also started focusing on other "frontier" areas.

In October 2020, the Russian prime minister said that Russia seeks to become a global leader in AI.[114] In November 2020, Russia announced it was setting up a quantum computing lab called the "National Quantum Laboratory" to build a quantum computer by 2024.[115] The more Russia invests in these areas, the more likely it is that the world will see new kinds of "vertical actions" from Russia on the world stage. But, more than anything else, the vertical world will force Russia to begin asking itself what it wants its future role to be. Does it want to be a counterweight to the US, China, and India? Does it want to recreate the Soviet Union? Or, does Russia want to unplug and look inward? After a long time, Russia can decide its fate, with and because of technology. Instead of being stuck to a status quo that came with energy exports or defense production, Russia can create its own status quo with technology.

For years, Russia was perceived to be in a period of resurgence, extending its reach worldwide. This analysis was premature. The true revival has not even begun yet. In the vertical world, the government in Moscow will be taking steps that will redefine and redesign Russia's footprint in the world. Through technology, a new Russia is forming that is less reliant on globalization. Through technology, a new Russia is developing that will resist any attempt to control it. A new Russia will have options that take Russia's economy and society in unimaginable directions through technology.

CHAPTER SIX

China And US Fight To Lead The World

Behind closed doors, globalization sometimes goes by another name: Americanization. That is because, to a certain degree, the current design of the world has been conceived by the US. The global institutions, systems, and rules that exist today, that have woven nations together over decades, were all created by the US. This means that, as countries bought into globalization, they were also buying into Americanization. Governments have designed their societies and economies around the US-led world. And, businesses have expanded and operated with the understanding that the US was in charge.

For many nations, the Americanized world is a comfortable status quo. But, for China, it has been captivity. The government in Beijing has bought into globalization because there has been no other option to develop and advance. Now, however, there is. Rapidly, with technology, China is unplugging from the established structures and is taking many nations with it. This is creating massive friction as China races to take control of the world and the US fights to keep control. At one end, China is using technology to replace globalization with something more China-centric. At another end, the US is using technology to re-Americanize the world and stop China's rise. As the US and China fight over technology, the world is splitting. The vertical world is forming as the US and China use technology to decide who calls the shots.

As this happens, both sides are realizing three things. First, the vertical world is inevitable because the era when a single superpower ruled the world is over.

The path of globalization, where a "single approach" was adopted by everyone else, has been marginalized. This means that the US can no longer remain the only leader. Now, the US and China are being forced to coexist with each other as superpowers. This is resulting in a "slice and dice" approach as the US and China compete for different territories and regions. Second, the vertical world is forming because nations are blocking out technology from the US or China. In some cases, governments are siding with the US, blocking out Chinese technology (and China). And, in other cases, governments are siding with China, blocking out US technology (and the US). Third, some countries are not comfortable aligning with either the US or China. They are using technology to build their own "corner" in the world.

While the vertical world is forming because of the actions of several nations, the rapid rise of the vertical world is a direct result of the fight between the US and China over technology. No longer is the US-China relationship being driven by traditional issues like the South China Sea or Taiwan. Now, at the center of the US-China relationship is technology. In the biggest fight for power since World War II, the US and China know technology is the key to victory. And, because of this, both sides are walling themselves off from one another in a way that is ripping the world apart and taking it in opposite directions.

Chinese Software, Algorithms Lock Out The US

For decades, China has depended on US software like Windows and Android. Even as China has become the global hardware leader, building the world's billions of devices, it continues to load US software onto everything it builds. Knowingly, China has been integrating the globe along a common fault line (US software) because there was no other choice. That is, until now. China has started launching its own software, including AI platforms, for the world to use. The world will soon revolve around predominantly two software ecosystems: one from the US and one from China. As China offers nations Chinese software, it represents a new "barrier" for the US. The Chinese software could end up locking out the US from parts of the world. The Chinese software could become a "wall" that stops the US from accessing certain nations.

The emergence of Chinese software is taking place in multiple areas. The first is mobile. For several years, Huawei has been working on its own OS called "HarmonyOS." It has been developed to replace Windows and Android. It is being designed as China works on a way to replace US technology - including software. For several years, China has been working on what is known as "3-5-2." This is a strategy to replace all foreign hardware and software by 2022 in three different phases: 30% of foreign technology removed by the end of 2020, 50% removed by the end of 2021, and the remaining 20% removed by the end of 2022.[116] This means, from Huawei to Xiaomi to ZTE to Oppo to Vivo, all Chinese devices will soon run Chinese software like HarmonyOS. Already, HarmonyOS has become the "unofficial" OS for China. Several Chinese companies are starting to integrate HarmonyOS into their products without "official orders" from Beijing. The moment Chinese firms had the opportunity to ditch US software, they took it. In November 2020, Midea, a Chinese appliance maker, announced a new line of smart home products, like dishwashers and stoves, powered entirely by HarmonyOS.[117] Before this, in July 2020, BYD, a Chinese carmaker, unveiled a new 5G-electric car that operates on HarmonyOS.[118] In June 2021, Huawei officially launched HarmonyOS on its smartphones, pledging that 100 devices will use the new OS.[119]

As China starts exporting devices with HarmonyOS, it is putting the US on notice. Until now, US technology firms, like Uber, Airbnb, and Amazon, have been operating on "friendly" OS to reach consumers, meaning American software like Android or iOS. Even when a consumer was using Uber on a Chinese device, that consumer was still using American software (i.e., Android) that Uber was loaded on. Going forward, as Chinese devices run HarmonyOS, a new reality emerges. To reach consumers around the world, US technology firms will be depending on Chinese software. For the first time, the business model of US firms will rely on the good grace of China. Take Africa. Currently, the biggest smartphone maker in Africa is Transsion, based in Shenzhen. It controls more than 50% of Africa's entire phone market (feature phones and smartphones).[120] Following China's "3-5-2" strategy, the next phones that Transsion sells will be loaded with Chinese software like HarmonyOS.

If most African consumers are using Chinese handsets loaded with the Chinese OS, it makes China the new gatekeeper for US technology companies. The next time the US and China clash, China could disable US technology companies, like Uber or Airbnb, from its OS. Now, in a flash, US firms will lose access to parts of Africa. Expand this to other parts of the world where Chinese devices dominate, and China suddenly controls what US businesses can or cannot do, especially the Silicon Valley firms. Through mobile OS, China could establish a new "barrier" to how US companies can access markets worldwide. Of course, the US might respond in kind. It could order Silicon Valley to shut out China. Arguably, this has already happened. In August 2020, the US ordered ByteDance to sell off some of its TikTok operations, including those in the US.[121] It was the first time the US had taken such an action against a Chinese technology company. It was a sign that Chinese technology firms may be locked out of the US market.

Another software front that China is working on is "AI brains." In January 2018, Alibaba exported a service called "City Brain" to Kuala Lumpur, Malaysia. This is an AI system that converts cities into smart cities. In Kuala Lumpur, it was tasked with handling traffic. And, within a short time, Malaysia announced it was rolling out City Brain across the nation. In the same period, Malaysia purchased Chinese facial recognition cameras for its police and also attracted US$1 billion from SenseTime to build an AI-park focused on research.[122] There is another way to look at this. It took decades for the US to take its technology worldwide and bring nations into its corner. With AI, it took less than two years for China to achieve the same in Malaysia, that is, bring Malaysia into China's orbit.

As China exports AI brains, it is exporting the new Chinese foundation for cities. This foundation may "support" other Chinese services from healthcare to education. This means that as cities adopt the Chinese smart city technologies, especially the AI brains, China may end up managing those cities. And, just like the mobile OS locking out the US, China's AI brains may integrate the Chinese services so that there is no role for the US to play in those cities. In fact, what can the US offer to Malaysia if Malaysian people are using China's AI brains for everything, from finance to entertainment to security? Alongside all of this, just as globalization allowed the US to take its ideals and culture to the world, so too, China's AI brains could allow China to do the same. The vertical world will not just be about whose technology nations are using, but also whose embedded cultures, beliefs, and ideals societies are using.

One way China can achieve this is through its corporate social credit system. This system, already online in China, gives corporations scores based on their "conduct." And, with these scores, corporations can and cannot do certain things. It is based on China's controversial social credit system, which is aimed at individuals. Once China begins exporting its corporate social credit system around the world, the system will act as a new "barrier" that restricts US companies from operating at their full potential. Many US firms could be given reduced scores (through AI bias), limiting what they can and cannot do in a specific city or market. This is the new business landscape facing US businesses in the vertical world.

The third software front that China is working on is AI avatars. These are advanced digital personas that mimic a real human being. They offer China another opportunity to make the world vertical. China has been deploying AI avatars mainly in media, allowing them to take over news broadcasts. But, China has also begun exporting these avatars abroad. In May 2019, Sogou, a Chinese technology company, signed a deal with Abu

Dhabi Media to create the world's first Arabic AI news anchor. It was designed to deliver the news in the United Arab Emirates (UAE).[123] And, it represents a challenge to US and Western media interests. Until recently, the US and its allies controlled the global media. This does not just include media outlets but also how these outlets tell a story (narrative). This has given the US and the West immense power. Now, with AI avatars, China is gaining a similar capability. With AI avatars, China can control whose news these avatars share. Whose reporting will the Chinese AI avatar in the UAE share: CNBC or Xinhua? This means that China's AI avatars could become a new "wall" that restricts Western media in certain parts of the world. Through AI avatars, the world could be split in an unprecedented way.

China Builds Its Own Navigation And Quantum Internet

A major pillar of the globalized world has been navigation. While certain regions, like the European Union (EU) and Russia, have their own navigation systems (i.e., Galileo and GLONASS respectively), most of the world uses the US navigation, known as the

"Global Positioning System" or "GPS." The US navigation system is the foundation the whole world has stood on for decades. At its core, GPS is an array of satellites that orbit the Earth. When someone uses GPS to move around, for instance, navigating a city's downtown, the device they are using (i.e., a smartphone or car navigation system) connects with multiple GPS satellites. The time it takes for their request to arrive at different satellites is how the GPS determines where the request is coming from. In more recent years, GPS applications have expanded to earthquake management and monitoring changing sea levels.[124]

Now, China has unveiled its rival to GPS. Some may view this as nothing significant, considering Europe and Russia already have their own navigation systems. But, there is a big difference: the European and Russian navigation systems were not exported to the world to rival GPS. With China, it is a different story. In July 2020, China's navigation system, known as the "BeiDou Navigation Satellite System" or just "BeiDou," gained global coverage with 35 satellites in space. It took China decades to reach this point, as the system has been in development since 1994.[125] Except, while China may have only finished its BeiDou system in July 2020, it had already exported the system to nations around the world. In August 2020, the number of countries that bought BeiDou reached 120, meaning that most of the world was already "customers" of China's navigation system.[126]

Equally important is that there is a crucial security difference between GPS and BeiDou. When it comes to GPS, the US navigation system is known as a "one-way communication system." This means that GPS is simply bouncing signals from a satellite to the source (i.e., a smartphone using Google Maps asking for directions in New York City). On the other hand, BeiDou is a two-way communication system. This means that BeiDou satellites can identify who is asking for navigation. This risk is so significant that Taiwan has warned that smartphones that are "BeiDou-enabled" may pose a national security risk because China can spy on the phones. Will nations ban BeiDou over security fears? These bans would represent new lines, blocking out Chinese technology.

In the vertical world, the big implication of BeiDou is that as it is rolled out, the world will split between two different navigation systems. In some parts of the world, BeiDou may be more popular than GPS and vice versa. This shift may already have happened. In

November 2020, new data showed that in the capital cities of 165 nations, BeiDou satellites were more active than GPS. Out of the 195 countries recognized by the United Nations, in 165 of those countries, China's navigation system was outmatching the US.[127] The split in navigation has already occurred, but it has not made headlines.

The competition between GPS and BeiDou will cause the vertical world to emerge at a grassroots level. Around the world, billions of people that use navigation will suddenly be using two very different systems. This is not just about optics. This is about the "ecosystems" that come with navigation. For example, GPS comes with many US services like mapping services and startups that require navigation capability (i.e., ride-sharing, food delivery). The same applies to services originating from China that are connected to China's BeiDou. This means that technology companies will now be "walled off" based on whose navigation system a nation is using. Or, nations might not be the ones making decisions. Instead, consumers who are making their choices, from ordering a taxi to finding directions, based on cost, accessibility, and options, will be deciding the fate of the US and China's navigation systems.

The US services and platforms that the world has grown with, which have created a "commonality" globally (everyone has been using the same services), will face new roadblocks and hurdles. The next generations of people in many parts of the world may grow up more accustomed to the Chinese brands and technology enabled by BeiDou than the US equivalent. This will pull them deeper into the Chinese world order and away from the American-led globalization.

China is also stepping out of the US-led world with a new form of the Internet. The current Internet in use today was developed by the US, and it has benefited the West in unprecedented ways. The US built the underwater cable network that carries 95% of the world's data and voice traffic. This has not only given complete control of the Internet traffic to the West, but it has also enabled Internet services, like Spotify and Netflix, to spread globally without any obstacles. And, of course, since the command-and-control centers of the Internet were all located in the US or allied Western nations, it gave the US unlimited leverage to gather intelligence and conduct surveillance on anybody anywhere in the world.

Now, China is pushing ahead with a plan of its own. First, like the US, a big part of China's plan to challenge the US-controlled Internet is to build the next generation of underwater cable networks. For example, China has built a cable connecting Brazil and Cameroon and a cable connecting Europe, Asia, and Africa.[128] This, of course, is raising eyebrows and causing "vertical decisions" - nations are trying to stop China from building these cables. In August 2019, Australia finished building an Internet cable called the "Coral Sea Cable" connecting the Solomon Islands and Papua New Guinea. Initially, Huawei was contracted to build this cable. But, after security concerns were raised, Australia stepped in.[129] In other words, Australia took a vertical decision, stopping the Chinese technology to keep certain regions, like the Pacific Islands, walled off from China and keep them within Australia's orbit.

Similarly, in June 2020, the US raised concerns after discovering that China partially built a new, direct cable connecting the US and Hong Kong.[130] A US committee demanded that this cable project be rejected. Before this, in February 2020, Facebook and Google, who were constructing the cable, filed paperwork to have other sections activated but not the section connecting Hong Kong and China.[131] Because of geopolitics, the strategies of Facebook and Google were changing.

Instead of including the whole world, now these companies accepted that certain nations and regions could not play a role in their connectivity plans.

While China's plans for the Internet are a big deal by itself, there is another area that shows equally incredible vertical thinking. It is to do with quantum computing. In August 2016, China launched a satellite, which is a part of a new quantum computing project called the "Quantum Experiments at Space Scale (QUESS)." This is a mission to build a Chinese quantum communications system in space. This system will allow China to beam the Internet down to Earth and encrypt traffic simultaneously. Just as the US built the world's underwater cable network, now, China is building the next such network in space using quantum computing.[132] In January 2018, China experimented with QUESS, successfully sending traffic between ground stations in China and Austria.[133] And, in January 2020, China conducted an experiment between QUESS and a mobile quantum ground station in China, successfully relaying encrypted data for almost eight minutes.[134]

As China plugs nations into BeiDou, it may soon start to plug nations into its quantum Internet too. This means that the US and China will be competing over who is supplying the world's Internet and who controls the world's data. Some nations will remain attached to the current Western-managed cables, but many others will join the Chinese-managed "space cables," fragmenting the world even further. At the same time, because China's QUESS satellites will be "encrypting" data, these satellites may also share data before encryption with China. This means the same surveillance capabilities the US has had for decades, that have given the US an edge in government relations and business negotiations, will now also be available to China. Will this give rise to a new Facebook coming from China? What will become of the business models of US technology firms that rely on collecting and processing data to drive their organizations?

With different nations connected to the Internet networks managed by two competitors, the Internet itself will become vertical. This means that through the Internet, the US and China could increasingly block each other out. It also means that, ironically, the vertical world will be ushered in from space. And, it is not just the satellites that are powering the quantum Internet. China is experimenting with other approaches as well. In January 2021, in an experiment by Chinese researchers, drones produced a "quantum connection" between two ground stations in China.[135] This means that China is developing the capabilities to create "hyperlocal" and on-demand quantum Internet networks. In the vertical world, how the Internet works or is structured increasingly has no relation to the past.

Digital Yuan Kicks Out USD From Markets

The end of the US dollar supremacy has been discussed for many years. But, the reality is, it has not happened. In fact, besides a few instances, such as Russia and China settling trade in local currencies, the rest of the world still trades in USD. Nobody has succeeded in making their currency a valid, global alternative. This could soon change. For the past several years, China has been quietly developing a "Digital Yuan," a "central bank digital currency" or "CBDC." Through this currency, China may be able to make its currency a genuine alternative to USD. However, it must be understood why USD became the global currency. This happened because of the circumstance the world was in after World War II. The US was the only remaining superpower. And, there was consensus (Bretton Woods) that USD should become the de facto reserve currency. These circumstances do not exist today for China. There has been no global conflict where China is left as the world's only superpower. And, there is no worldwide consensus that China's Yuan (digital or physical) should replace USD. In other words, the current state of the world is entirely different.

And, because the circumstances are different, China will have to chart a new path to take its Digital Yuan around the world. To achieve this, China has multiple irons in the fire. First, China is leveraging its startups to take Digital Yuan to nations. One of the startups is Didi, China's equivalent of Uber. In July 2020, Didi announced it would be taking part in a trial of China's CBDC - making the digital currency a new dominant payment method for Didi's 500 million users (in China).[136] In December 2020, China held a trial where it gave away US$3.1 million worth of Digital Yuan to 100,000 residents of Suzhou, a Chinese city located northwest of Shanghai. Residents that received the money were able to use it for many services, including Didi.[137] And, in June 2021, the capital city of Beijing announced a similar initiative, giving away US$6.2 million to residents in a lottery.[138] It is not surprising that

China wants startups like Didi to use Digital Yuan. It is a fast way for the currency to gain traction domestically.

But, Didi is a global company. It already operates in Latin America. And, in February 2021, Didi said it plans to enter parts of Western Europe, specifically the United Kingdom, Germany, and France.[139] This means, as Didi goes global, it might take Digital Yuan with it, injecting it into markets all over the world. This will increase the adoption of China's digital currency faster, and in a way the world has never seen before. To incentivize people outside of China to use Digital Yuan, Didi's app could offer 10% or 15% off if a ride is paid for in China's digital currency. Of course, some may object to settling in a foreign currency, especially a digital currency, but consider the ease that digital currencies can be purchased. In February 2021, when the cryptocurrency Dogecoin made headlines, people could buy the currency in a matter of seconds via online platforms. This same ease could exist with purchasing Digital Yuan. Except, Didi is more than just a ride-hailing service. It also offers financing and food delivery. It is an entire ecosystem of services hailing from China. From Budapest to Bengaluru, tens of millions of people may use Didi to move around, eat food or get money.

Every transaction, including financing, may be conducted in Digital Yuan. And equally importantly, instead of the financial institutions driving the currency, China's CBDC will be taking off at a grassroots level, via millennials and Gen Z engaging with the sharing economy (like ride-sharing).

A second iron in the fire is that China has begun to work directly with US allies. In February 2021, China's central bank, the People's Bank of China (PBoC), signed a deal to work with the United Arab Emirates (UAE) and Thailand, settling cross-border payments in digital currencies. This is a veiled shot at USD, which is currently the de facto cross-border payment method. The fact that the UAE is willing to explore settling certain transactions in China's digital currency points to the US "control" weakening over the world. And, it is a sign that as China takes its Digital Yuan to nations, economies will split along multiple currency lines. Instead of USD being the only preferred currency, China's Digital Yuan may also claim a similar position.

The third iron in the fire is that China is gaining direct control of critical payment systems. After the Chinese government announced a crackdown on large technology firms in 2020, in January 2021, Beijing announced a new model for Ant Group. This company is behind some of China's most extensive payment processing systems. One of the proposals was for Ant Group to be controlled by PBoC. This would mean that China would have unfettered access to Ant Group, including deciding what currencies Ant Group pushes. Why does this matter? Because, in September 2020, Ant Group announced a new blockchain-based cross-border payment system. Put differently, Ant Group has created a new system to settle payments between different nations. By taking control of Ant Group, China can install "Digital Yuan" as the new way for countries using Ant Group's system to settle payments and trade.

These three strategies, in conjunction, are giving nations new currency options. Before, the US and Western currencies were prioritized not just because the global systems revolved around them but also because they were secure and accessible. So far, this is not the case for China's Digital Yuan. The world does not revolve around Yuan, nor is it easily accessible (or in-demand). With technology, China can now take Digital Yuan to the whole world in strategic ways. As Chinese services are adopted, Digital Yuan will ride in on them, creating a sense of "security" that Digital Yuan can be trusted.

It is unlikely that nations will outright pick Digital Yuan over USD. But, what is likely is that economies will be split along these new vertical lines. As businesses and consumers use Digital Yuan, the US currency will lose its "king" status, and China's currency will become integrated into the world. At the same time, some nations could take steps to restrict access to either currency, erecting new barriers because of technology. The emergence of China's Digital Yuan could result in new technology-based walls emerging as nations struggle to deal with the implications of two currencies fighting for global supremacy.

China Splits Global Finance Along Vertical Lines

Finance has been a driving force connecting and integrating nations. The world has revolved around a handful of Western financial epicenters that drive all the money and attention. This has meant that investment, from large institutional investors to average individuals, has flowed in a particular direction (to cities like New York, London, or Tokyo). It has also meant that global finance and globalization have gone hand-in-hand. That is, without getting rid of economic barriers, the stock markets cannot function freely. And, without stock markets, one of the most efficient ways of moving capital worldwide and connecting economies will not exist.

Because of the role technology is playing in the world, this model is being disrupted. Now, a more vertical model is emerging, where global finance is split along new national boundaries. Since February 2017, the US has been aiming at Chinese technology firms, threatening to delist them from the US stock markets. And, the US has also warned that Chinese investment in critical US startups is a geopolitical risk. By taking action on stock markets, the US is trying to push Chinese money out of its economy and also protect the US edge from being handed over to China (through Chinese investments in US companies). Now, many Chinese technology firms are rethinking their global strategy to raise money. The US and Western stock markets have become too risky for them.

As a result, China is taking vertical steps to disconnect and reduce reliance on the US and Western financial centers. China is creating its own financial independence through technology. In July 2019, the Chinese government launched the "Science and

Technology Innovation Board," or "STAR Market," on the Shanghai Stock Exchange (SSE).[140] This is China's attempt to build its own Nasdaq. And it is part of China's vision of becoming self-sufficient in technology. In August 2020, more than a year after the STAR Market launched, Ant Group announced it was listing on STAR Market and the Hong Kong Stock Exchange (HKSE) - a dual listing.[141] It was expected to be the largest IPO in the world, and it drew almost US$3 trillion in bids[142] (ultimately, the IPO was suspended in November 2020). [143] Ant's IPO was a sign that billion-dollar companies are prepared to go public in China over the US, a move that was unthinkable just a few years ago. In March 2021, Baidu, often referred to as the Google of China, made a secondary listing in Hong Kong.[144] This was a strategic move by one of China's biggest technology companies to reduce its dependence on the US financial markets.

The way global finance has been working is changing. It is becoming vertical. The two largest economies in the world, the US and China, are actively trying to reduce their reliance on each other when it comes to investments. The US is becoming deeply cautious and concerned about Chinese investments. And

China does not want the US money out of fear that if it accepts those investments, then Chinese firms will be held hostage. It is a lose-lose situation. It is a significant shift from the past. In the short term, this will hurt China, considering how deep the Western pockets are. But, the vertical decisions that China is taking today may benefit China in the long term. How? At one end, the US is cutting off China, threatening investors and corporations worldwide who have invested in China or are used to moving capital freely. But, as China is cut off, it is building financial capabilities out of US control. And, this could begin to take investment away from the US and Western stock markets. The US and the West's grip on the movement of capital will be weakened because of the vertical world. On top of that, the future China will be insulated from US geopolitics in a new way as its technology firms will not be intensely reliant on the US and Western financial world.

The many Chinese technology firms that exist today (and will emerge tomorrow) may be more dependent on China than the US for their financing. This is a new paradigm for China and the world. At the same time, China could use its technology-focused stock markets to push other nations to "unplug" from the US.

For example, China could become an "IPO hub" by offering private companies a base stock price if they list on the market. This means, if a biotechnology firm from Nigeria lists on the STAR Market, regardless of how the stock performs when it goes public, China will ensure a specific base price - guaranteed by the Chinese state-owned banks. This will represent the direct involvement of the Chinese government in the performance of a foreign IPO. Is the US government prepared to take a similar stance in US stock markets to keep investment? This will fundamentally change the modus operandi of the West, where the government stays out of the affairs of financial markets unless there is a crisis. Except, even here, this approach is already changing. In February 2021, the UK announced a new venture fund that would give the government a stake - like a board seat - in startups. In the West, to compete with China, governments are becoming board members of new companies. Does this make these companies the same as the state-run companies that the West has criticized China over for decades? To compete with China in the vertical world, is the West taking a page out of China's playbook?

Because technology is playing such a monumental role in defining the future of nations, new restrictions are emerging around the movement of capital. The vertical world means that money cannot flow freely anymore. This changes how global finance works. The next barriers to capital movements are not coming through capital controls or currency devaluation. Instead, they are coming through stock markets and investments increasingly being cut off from one another and politicized. This not only means that stock markets are becoming disconnected from one another, it also means that existing investments could be in jeopardy as nations aim at technology companies. Without the free movement of capital, globalization grinds to a halt. How can globalization truly be achieved if investors cannot access the most important markets around the world?

At the same time, the Western financial systems that underpin the world could face new challenges in the form of Chinese blockchain. Currently, the single most important financial system in the world is called "SWIFT." It stands for the "Society for Worldwide Interbank Financial Telecommunication." SWIFT acts as a "network" for money to be sent and received by banks worldwide. If a person in Tel Aviv wants to send

US$1,000 to someone in Paris, this transaction passes through SWIFT. In other words, SWIFT represents a global system that the whole world uses. It enables the movement of capital across the globe, uniformly integrating economies. And, because SWIFT is led by the US and is based in Europe, it gives the West tremendous control over global finance.

For some nations, this has been a risk. In September 2014, as tensions between the US and Russia rose, the US threatened to remove Russian banks from SWIFT. This drew an immediate rebuke from Russia.[145] If this happened, it would have crippled the Russian economy. Because of this risk, for several years, Russia, along with the BRICS (Brazil, Russia, India, China, and South Africa), have proposed an alternative to SWIFT.[146][147] However, these ideas never gained global traction, even as the prototypes (alternative systems to SWIFT) were developed. That is, except for China (and separately Russia). Over the past several years, China has been quietly developing its alternative to SWIFT. It is called "CIPS," or the "Cross-Border Inter-Bank Payments System." This is the system that underpins China's domestic banks. And China has begun taking it to the world to "unplug" nations from SWIFT.

In August 2020, China planned to have 1,000 international stakeholders join CIPS by the end of the year.[148] There is another part of China's plan to take on SWIFT that has received less attention. It is called the "Blockchain Services Network" or "BSN." And, it is a new wiring for the world economy, including finance. It has been compared to the Internet in that global activity could soon take place on BSN, a system controlled entirely by China. If a Spanish startup wants to sell goods to consumers in Thailand, it would use BSN. Or, if the Chilean government wants to share data with South Africa, it would use BSN. The BSN is a holistic solution for everything. Of course, pegging an entire economy to a Chinese system will not sit well with the US, or even India, Japan, or Australia. This will be a non-starter. Some nations will be using China's BSN for capital movements, e-commerce, or data sharing, while others will be using opposite systems. The adoption of blockchains from different nations will divide the world in unprecedented ways. It will lead to "political blockchains" - blockchains that revolve around different ideologies and geopolitics. In the vertical world, finance will take on a brand new appearance. It will be split along ideological lines, all because of technology.

With Chips, China Gains Independence From The US

While China seeks technology independence from the US, it is still heavily reliant on the US for specific technologies, none more than chips. Chips are the brains that are powering every ambition China has with technology. This dependency has made China aware of how captive it is in the current global design of the world. That is because, when tensions with the US (or the West) have flared, the US used globalization to punish China.

For example, throughout 2020, as technology became the most significant factor affecting US-China relations, the US went after Chinese technology companies. One of these companies, Huawei, became blacklisted by the US. The US forced companies who were exporting chips to Huawei to get permission from the US first. This essentially cut Huawei's access to chips and negatively impacted the company. In November 2020, Huawei announced it would be selling Honor, a lower-end smartphone division, because it had lost access to advanced chips and was prioritizing higher-end smartphones.[149] This is the risk that China faces if it remains plugged into the current globalized world.

Under the current model of globalization, the success of China and its companies will remain dependent on whether the US approves what China is doing.

So, for the government in China, long-term success and security requires a vertical chip industry. To build its chips, China is pouring billions into its national semiconductor company, "Semiconductor Manufacturing International Corporation (SMIC)." In July 2020, SMIC announced a US$7.6 billion deal with the "Beijing Economic-Technological Development Area (BDA)," a state-led economic zone, to build wafers (used to produce integrated circuits on the semiconductor). It would result in more than US$2 billion in state funds being invested in SMIC.[150] And, in the same month, SMIC also said it wanted to raise up to US$7.5 billion through the Chinese stock markets.[151] At the same time, more than 100 engineers from TSMC, the world's largest chip production company based in Taiwan, have been poached by China to work on various projects funded by the government.[152]

Alongside this, while China may be behind in certain kinds of semiconductors, it is ahead in next-generation semiconductors. One company in China developing semiconductors is "Horizon Robotics." It is developing "AI on a chip." Horizon's objective is to allow products with AI in chips to operate offline (without the Internet connection). While China may be dependent on the US in the old world of semiconductors, China is acting vertically from the start in the new arenas. Once China develops a Chinese chip industry that can match the US (along with Israel and South Korea), the "psyche" of the world will change.

This means, instead of nations only thinking about the US when it comes to chips, they will also begin to think of China. When China can build its chips, investments, commercial deals, and procurement will also shift. Instead of everything going one way as it has in the globalized world (i.e., towards the US), it will split into multiple directions.

At the same time, once China builds its chips, it could take radical steps to shrink the US footprint. For example, could China make its chips "exclusive"? This means Chinese chips would only work with Chinese hardware and software. In other words, US technology firms would be locked out of supplying components to devices that use Chinese chips. Or, China can go beyond this and start forcing foreign products to use Chinese chips. When German or Japanese automakers export vehicles to the Chinese market, they might have to install Chinese chips, removing US chips from the equation.

These moves, which could be amplified as China takes its products worldwide, would limit the role that the US plays in the global technology sector. Companies around the world will face a new predicament: to access China or markets that China controls, they will have to unplug from the US technologies. Unlike in the past, when companies picked the US to gain unfettered access to the world, now, choosing the US could mean losing access and revenue. For the first time, as the US and China clash, globalization may act as a barrier to the success of many firms. Companies will be forced to pick sides, either aligning with China to sell to consumers or supporting the US and losing access to consumers.

There may also be "creative ways" China can speed up its chip development. One of China's big "nuclear cards" is to weaponize access to its domestic market for companies like Apple. China may force Apple to become its new chip supplier to Chinese companies if it wants to operate in China. The Cupertino-based firm depends heavily on the Chinese market for revenue (in some years, Apple's China revenue accounted for 25% of its global revenue). And, for years, Apple has been steadfast in developing its own proprietary chips for its devices, replacing Intel chips. Could China force Apple (or even Samsung) to make chips for firms like Huawei and Xiaomi or lose access to the Chinese market? An ultimatum like this would be tricky to navigate. The US government, of course, will disagree with Apple producing chips for China and with China weaponizing its market access. But, Apple, and its entire ecosystem of suppliers and app developers, may panic at the very notion of losing access to the Chinese market. The vertical world will push large companies into crisis mode as new challenges that they have not imagined suddenly emerge.

In 2019, China spent over US$300 billion on chips. This was US$62 billion more than what China spent on oil.[153] In other words, China is already spending more on chips than energy because of how chips will power the future that China is building for itself and the world.

Global Division Over Whose Technology Rules To Follow

Globalization has meant that the world followed the same rules. And, because the US has led the world, it meant that the world was following the US rules. This was a singular approach to globalization. It gave the US and its allies tremendous power. It meant that every nation was on the same page. There was a "one size fits all" approach. Now, in the vertical world, this is no longer the case. China has begun building its own technology rules that challenge the US-led model. This will lead to the world being split over whose technology rules nations (and regions) use. And, most surprisingly, China may take its technology rules to the world through US institutions!

In December 2019, new documents revealed that Chinese technology firms, like ZTE and China Telecom, had been quietly designing facial recognition rules for the UN's "International Telecommunication Union (ITU)." In the past, the ITU's rules were implemented in hundreds of nations[154]. It is also important to note that many ITU member countries are also members of China's "One Belt, One Road (OBOR)" initiative.

OBOR is China's strategy to redesign global trade. In other words, when it comes to technology rules in the vertical world, China is operating on two fronts. On one front, it is building its own technology for the world to use (i.e., chips, smartphones, or 5G) that blocks out the US. On the other front, it is designing the very rules that will affect how Chinese technology functions and the role the US plays in the world.

As China takes its technology rules to the world, directly to nations, or through the "global" institutions, countries will face a challenge they have not encountered before. Whose rules should they adopt? In the past, there were "single rules" that every nation followed. From AI to 6G, the US and China will offer different rules to countries. The more nations pick sides, the more the world will split as new fault lines will emerge.

Different rules mean that technology might behave differently, like the US algorithms caring more about certain biases than the Chinese algorithms. At the same time, because technology companies are building the rules, these companies will have an unfair advantage: they will be developing practices that might benefit their products and services. This is akin to social media firms creating the rules for net neutrality. What kind of rules would be created?

A similar vertical split is emerging with 5G. The forum that sets the global telecommunications rules is known as "3GPP" and comprises several smaller organizations. When it comes to 5G, Huawei has been proposing more rules than any other company, including its competitors like Nokia and Ericsson. If China succeeds in influencing 3GPP, then a new reality emerges. At a certain point, China's influence over the US-led institutions, like the UN, may become so great that the US (and its allies) can do nothing else but move on from those institutions. This means the vertical world may not just be about China exiting the US world order, but also, in some instances, the US exiting its creations, like the UN, because it has lost control and dominance.

Because the US and China are fundamentally different from one another, from political ideology to economic design, the technology rules that both sides create will also be fundamentally different. The world will soon have two competing frameworks for technology governance. The old dream of globalization, where there is a single, global approach to an issue, like technology, is rapidly disappearing. The US will have its standards, and China will have its own. The dozens of other nations, from Japan to Australia to Ethiopia, will either have to act vertically and create their own rules or pick somebody else's side. This will further fracture the world. Instead of standard rules integrating nations, the new regulations to govern technology will soon become a source of divergence and disunion.

Conclusion

For a long time, questions about who will rule the world depended on who would win in a nuclear exchange. This scenario was seen as the only way for a new power to emerge in the world. It was assumed, especially by the US and its allies, that not only would they remain in charge. But, through globalization, they could manage non-Western nations who had superpower ambitions. The West never imagined that to become a superpower, a country might discard the playbook of globalization and try something new. After all, the few nations that tried this ended up on the periphery of the world, struggling for basic survival.

With China, the old ideas and ideals are being tossed aside. With technology, China is imagining a new world, where control and power do not lie only with the US. The world is slowly becoming divided by nations choosing technology supplied by China over the US or vice-versa. And, these are not technologies that "complement" what already exists. China is not exporting only cloud computing systems that sit on top of the US-controlled Internet. The technology systems that China has begun exporting are holistic alternatives to what the US has created.

For many nations, choosing the US or Chinese technology is a vertical paradox. On the one hand, it is "one or the other" (i.e., Indonesia purchasing systems from Amazon or Alibaba). But, on the other hand, it is "one and the other" (i.e., Brazil following the US and Chinese technology rules). Some nations will be explicit in choosing sides. But, many others will see no benefit in taking a firm position. Instead, they will try and play both sides, allowing technology to come in from all directions. And, as this happens, they will be split internally, as different technologies try to block each other out. As the US and China compete in the vertical world, technology will increasingly be viewed as an extension of nations. It will no longer just be US corporations taking products and services to the world. Behind them, the shadow of the US government will be visible, supporting and steering its companies to achieve specific objectives. This is eerily reminiscent of what China has been doing to help its companies expand. And, it means, in the vertical world, the US behavior might, at times, mimic China.

However, for both the US and China, the biggest challenge they will face is not fighting each other but convincing other nations to join their side. If technology allows governments to act independently, why should countries join the US or China? Instead, nations are likely to try and build their own sides, independent of the big powers. And, this means that while the US and China take their technology to the world to block each other out, these same technologies may end up blocking out the US and China. Nations may use technology to carve out their own space in the world.

As the US and China compete to lead the world, the systems that have integrated nations will be cut down. Either China will outright leave them, or the US will take steps to limit China's power. The stability and conformity that globalization has created will disappear. As the US and China act with one objective, to outcompete the other through technology, the whole world will be shaken. The design underpinning the world for decades has started to disappear. A new design is now emerging as two superpowers fight for technological supremacy and try to remake the world in their image.

CHAPTER SEVEN

Unshackling Of Japan

While the US (and Western Europe) were the architects of globalization, nations like Japan made globalization "real." After World War II, as Japan rebuilt itself into one of the largest economies in the world, it put globalization at the center of its design. This meant the more Japanese goods and brands dominated markets worldwide, the more globalization was "felt" by countries and billions of consumers. From cars to televisions to cameras, it was the Japanese goods that woke people up to a new reality: the barriers that once divided the world were disappearing.

Except, as Japan bought into globalization, it was not love at first sight. The government in Tokyo took a cautious approach. At one moment, Japan went all in when it came to exporting goods around the world. But, at another moment, when it came to local economy and society, Japan blocked globalization. It did not allow foreign goods, brands, or practices to dominate its economy and society. And, then, because of Japan's alliance with the US, Japan never questioned how globalization was functioning, from institutions to global decisions.

Now, with technology, Japan is asserting itself in new ways. The Japan that the world has known is rapidly fading away. A new Japan is rising. Whatever Japan relied on globalization for, such as economic growth or geopolitical power, it is now quickly using technology to achieve on its own. The "threads" that have woven Japan into the world, and made it reliant on specific global systems and nations, are now becoming loose. The way Japan is turning to technology is fracturing the very structure of the world, from energy to international relations. At the same time, Japan's vertical transformation is taking place amidst a massive metamorphosis in the Indo-Pacific. The status quo that Japan developed under, where the US called the shots, is now being shattered by nations like China and Russia. The US "shadow" that protected Japan for decades is now taking a different form, and Japan's place (and fate) is now in question.

But, in Japan's modern journey with globalization, the biggest misunderstanding has been that Japan's actions on the world stage, in support of globalization, came from a place of acceptance. That Japan's desires and wants are precisely the same as that of the West. This is wrong. Japan has been compliant because it has had no choice. It was globalization or isolation. Now, with technology, Japan is finding new roots. It is re-establishing a connection with who it really is. And, the steps it is taking will challenge the models and masters it has followed for so long.

Japan's Vertical Relationships With The US, India

Since the end of World War II, Japan has depended on the US for its defense needs. The US has acted as a "protective umbrella," stopping other nations from taking aggressive steps towards Japan. And, by protecting Japan, the US gained a "foothold" in the Indo-Pacific, a way to counter competitors like China and Russia. Except, there is an inconvenient truth. This relationship has never been equal. Although Japan and the US have had a military partnership for decades, Washington has always had the upper hand. The power imbalance was clear. This imbalance resulted in Japan never having to invest in its own military. Why? Because there was no incentive for Japan to protect itself when the US was there to do that job. In the Indo-Pacific, nobody could fight the US.

Today, the situation in the Indo-Pacific has dramatically changed. Nations like China and Russia have built sophisticated militaries and modernized their defenses. The gap between the US military and its competitors is closing fast. The idea that nobody can fight the US may not be accurate in the future. The emergence of stronger American adversaries is putting pressure on Japan to take matters into its own hands. This is turning Japan into a new military power. In September 2020, the Japanese defense ministry proposed a US$51.9 billion defense budget, the highest such defense budget in Japan in more than 20 years.[155] At the center of Japan's defense strategy are emerging technologies like unmanned systems.

As the government in Tokyo invests in these areas, it is stepping into the vertical world. In some ways, it is becoming a vertical military power - a nation that is not reliant on others for its military needs. In November 2018, Japan announced it would boost investments in AI and unmanned systems to offset a manpower shortage in its military.[156] A few months earlier, in August 2018, Japan began testing "pre-crime" AI to predict terrorist attacks and the behavior of foreign ships.[157] By the 2030s, Japan wants to have its own homegrown stealth fighter jet. And, during the same period, the Japanese Air Self-Defense Force (JASDF) wants autonomous drones flying alongside manned fighter jets to carry out missions.[158]

These initiatives may appear small and scattered. But, behind them is a powerful shift: many defense needs that Japan once turned to the US for could soon be handled by Japan on its own through technology. As a result, the old Japan - that was "plugged" into the US - is getting redesigned. As Japan's investments in the next-generation defense technologies grow, Japan will have its own military power for the first time in decades. This will allow Japan to take action it could not have taken independently before. In fact, through technology, Japan may attain military independence and make decisions that affect the very globalized world that has made Japan an economic powerhouse. For example, in January 2019, Japan unveiled plans to develop submarines that use AI to collect data.[159] In the future, these submarines could be armed and used by Japan to escort its cargo vessels - from automotive exports to energy - traveling throughout the Indo-Pacific. Instead of relying on the US for keeping its ships safe, through AI, Japan could take matters into its own hands.

In other words, Japan building a new military and achieving "defense" independence will be a "barrier" to the US and globalization. It means that Japan could start taking independent military action and may not need the global systems the way it once did.

As Japan builds a vertical military, it is also approaching relationship-building differently. Instead of integrating with the whole world, Japan is becoming selective about who it wants its economic and geopolitical future tied to. Take Japan's relationship with India. From bullet trains to solving pollution, Japan is working with India on multiple fronts. But, two fronts, in particular, are driving "selective relations," an aspect of the vertical world. The first front is military robots. In January 2018, Japan and India unveiled a new partnership to jointly develop AI and military robots for the military. The first project will develop an unmanned ground vehicle (UGV).[160] To influence the future of the Indo-Pacific, Japan and India are not relying on established defense blocs. Instead, they are building a one-on-one relationship built entirely around emerging technologies.

The second front is AI. In December 2019, the leader of SoftBank called Japan "underdeveloped" in AI and called for massive investments in the field. Among the many proposals was creating an "AI platform" that would connect Japan with India and Southeast Asia to bolster economic growth.[161]

While SoftBank's proposal is not the official foreign policy of Japan, it shows how Japan's private sector is thinking. The same businesses that once wanted to enter every market are now becoming extremely selective. The

Japanese business community is starting to think vertically. A new "AI connection" between Japan and India represents an exclusive technology corridor in the region. As this develops, it means two of the largest economies in the Indo-Pacific will no longer be "linked" using the established, globalized channels. Through AI, Japan and India may be integrated on their own independent axis.

Using Solar Power, Japan Replaces The Middle East

One of the big reasons why Japan adopted globalization had to do with energy. Around 90% of Japan's oil is imported, meaning that Tokyo's access to energy would be restricted without global rules and integration. Hence, because Japan relied on foreign energy, mainly from the Middle East, the Japanese foreign policy has been designed a certain way. The government in Tokyo has either remained neutral on various global issues, or if it aligned with the West, it did so in a way so that the energy flows were not disrupted. In short, the more Japan had to rely on importing oil from overseas, the more reliant Japan was on globalization.

But, what if Japan could build its energy supply at home? In April 2014, the Japanese Aerospace Exploration Agency (JAXA), Japan's space agency, proposed a solar power farm in space. Using a combination of mirrors and solar panels, solar power would be sent from space, down to Japan and converted into electricity.[162] It would supply power to towns and industries. If achieved, JAXA's plan would represent solar power on steroids. At the same time, in October 2020, the Japanese government announced a pledge to become carbon neutral by 2050. To achieve this, Japan will invest heavily in local renewable and clean energy sources.[163]

These initiatives point to Japan cutting its reliance on foreign energy. And, in the process, it is cutting one of its most extensive connections to globalization. Through technology, Japan no longer needs the global systems the way it once did. Instead, Japan could soon be satisfying its energy needs right at home. This means that the entire international energy trade could be disrupted as nations, like Japan, use technology to create local energy farms. And, as countries solve their energy challenges locally, what they build, from solar power farms to clean energy grids, will also act as barriers, reducing their integration with the rest of the world. These nations will become "self-sufficient" in energy

The more Japan takes vertical steps around energy, the faster it could become an energy producer. And, it may, like other energy-producing nations, start exporting power to other countries. This might lead to a new area of competition for Japan. In March 2016, China unveiled plans for a US$50 trillion global energy grid that would utilize solar power and other new forms of energy. The grid would connect all the regions of the world and could be ready by 2050.[164] The Chinese energy grid represents a new energy framework for the world, challenging the Western and Middle Eastern control over global energy supplies.

However, unlike China, Japan may not want to export energy to the whole world (or may not be able to). Just as Japan's foreign policy is becoming selective, so too, Japan's energy exports may be selective, only for the like-minded nations. One such group of nations could be the "QUAD Alliance" made up of the US, Japan, India, and Australia. This would be a massive, vertical step. A group of nations would be connecting themselves to a new, exclusive energy grid to bolster national security. At the same time, these nations may "unplug" from the traditional energy grids operated by Saudi Arabia or Russia. And, on top of all this, Japan could export the solar power technology, allowing many nations to become energy independent, like those in Africa.

The same driving force, energy, which has been driving nations to globalize and integrate, may soon push countries like Japan to act vertically. Instead of the whole world depending on a few energy epicenters, soon there may be dozens of energy epicenters, each catering to a different group of nations. Alongside all this, for Japan, sourcing its own energy locally could lead to a new, vertical foreign policy. When Tokyo no longer needs the Middle East for energy or the US to protect Japanese energy imports, Japan may make different decisions on the world stage. Instead of aligning with its traditional allies, Japan may stay quiet or diverge completely. When Japan is no longer worried about its energy supplies being affected, it may go unhinged.

Just as energy has driven globalization in the past, it will do so in the future too. Except, this time, it will be a different story. Instead of integrating the whole world, energy will cause nations to diverge from one another. The next era of energy exports will follow a vertical path.

Attempting To Wall Off Japan's Economy From China

In May 2020, the US unveiled a new group called the "Economic Prosperity Network." It is made up of US allies like Australia, India, Japan, New Zealand, South Korea, and Vietnam, who, in conjunction, are looking to move supply chains out of China.[165] One of the first nations to sign onto this was Japan. Even before the US proposed this group, Japan was already taking steps to reduce its economic integration with China. Months before the Economic Prosperity Network was proposed, Japan announced a plan in March 2020 to move supply chains out of China.[166] In July 2020, the Japanese government announced a plan to help 87 Japanese firms move manufacturing out of China - or what is known as "Chexit." The companies will receive US$653 million in total to move manufacturing to Japan or Southeast Asia.[167]

Shortly after this, in September 2020, Japan announced a further US$221 million for Japanese firms to move manufacturing to other countries, specifically India or Bangladesh.[168] More broadly, Japan is looking at the movement of supply chains to develop better relations with the Association of Southeast Asian Nations (ASEAN).

And, the Japanese business community is responding in kind. In December 2020, a survey conducted in Japan found that 40% of technology companies are already in the process of moving supply chains out of China.[169] A separate survey conducted in March 2020 found that 80% of Japanese firms are already overhauling their supply chains because of the pandemic and concerns about China.[170] And, in June 2020, Panasonic was in the final stages of shifting production of its home appliances from China to Indonesia.[171]

Except, while some Japanese technology firms are rethinking their Chinese footprint, others are deepening their investments in China. This is splitting the Japanese business community as Japan tries to act vertically. In March 2021, Fanuc, the world's largest producer of automation equipment, announced a US$240 million investment in China, its largest such investment.[172] In April 2020, Sony invested US$400 million in Bilibili, often referred to as the "YouTube of China."[173] And, in November 2020, Shionogi, a Japanese pharmaceutical company, inked two healthcare data deals with Ping An, one of China's largest insurance companies.[174] Most surprisingly, Japan-China collaboration in technology has entered areas that the Japanese government might not be comfortable with. In November 2020, Tencent began helping Toyota identify cyber vulnerabilities in its cars.[175] Are Japanese car companies depending on Chinese technology for cybersecurity? At the same time, many Japanese businesses continue to export data overseas. In a survey conducted in May 2021, 40% of respondents said they store customer data outside of Japan, including in China.[176] Of course, some Japanese technology companies are not thinking twice about moving their data from China. In March 2021, after it was revealed that China accessed Japanese user data, the Japanese messaging app Line moved all data from China to Japan.[177]

What is taking place in Japan is a challenge many nations will face as they try to act vertically. The Japanese government has a vision (not being reliant on China) but industry has different aspirations. And, the most critical sector that will decide whether a vision can be achieved or not is the technology industry. As Japan moves in this new direction of reducing integration with China, it is challenging globalization. Japan is trying to unplug from the largest economy in the Indo-Pacific. This is opposite to how nations have operated in the past. When it comes to economic integration, especially around supply chains and critical technology, countries like Japan want to cut themselves off from the epicenters like China. For Japan, it is either bringing businesses home or sending them to other nations that it can lead.

As Japan and its allies move supply chains out of China, the global economy will change. For decades, supply chains have quietly driven globalization. They have integrated economies, given rise to labor movements, and enabled multinationals to flourish. Now, when it comes to supply chains, especially those around technology, a different paradigm has emerged. Nations like Japan are becoming extremely concerned about who they want their supply chains structured around. This divides the world. It means that the current and future supply chains will now follow a vertical path, as different supply chains revolve around other nations. The uniformity of the past is gone

At the same time, while Japan tries to reduce its economic integration with China, the Japanese government is attempting to build other critical technology sectors that are not dependent on China from the get-go. One of these sectors is rare earth minerals. These minerals are essential for high-tech goods. And China controls them, supplying over 85% of the world's rare earth minerals.[178] This is creating fears in other nations, like Japan, that China could cut off the flow of these minerals if tensions flare. To counter this, in August 2020, Japan announced new investments in rare earth minerals to reduce dependency on China. These investments will see Japan gaining control of rare earth mines in other nations and building more domestic capabilities to process the raw materials.[179] When it comes to sourcing the materials for future Japanese goods, Japan is acting vertically. From self-driving cars to smartphones, the next Japanese products might all have Japanese rare earth minerals, not Chinese. If Japan can become a hub for rare earth minerals, then other parts of the world may shift away from China and become more "Japan-centric," too. This represents a new kind of technology-based fault line. Some areas of the world may use China for their rare earth needs, while others may use Japan. And Japan has a good chance at becoming a hub for rare earth minerals. In December 2018, geologists found a rare earth mineral deposit off the coast of Japan that could satisfy global demand for "centuries." The deposit is so rich that one mineral, yttrium, could be mined for the next 780 years.[180]

Conclusion

Nations like Japan have held globalization together. Without the world's most important powers, like Japan, buying into globalization, the modern design of the world would have likely collapsed a long time ago. This collapse is what is beginning today. For years, Japan may have had buyer's remorse. But, it had no choice. Now, it is taking steps to exchange what it has bought for decades for something different - something vertical. In the most critical areas, like defense, energy, and geopolitics, the government in Tokyo is using technology to act independently and regain control over areas it has long let other nations dominate.

What will a vertical Japan mean for the world? In a nutshell: loss of stability. The decisions Japan has made have helped keep the world on a specific trajectory. As one of the largest economies, Japan's decisions have mattered. The rest of the world has viewed what Japan has done, from economy to exports, as an indicator of whether a situation was improving or worsening. Now, this model is fading away. The government in Tokyo is no longer making decisions or formulating strategies to keep the world moving in a particular direction. Now, it is acting from a vertical place. And, as the rest of the world watches what Japan is doing, they will see it as an indicator that the current form of globalization is no longer working. If Japan is willing to approach globalization in a new way, why should the rest of the world remain attached to the old way?

What Japan is doing is fundamentally different than what the US, European Union (EU), China, or India are doing. That is because the US and EU designed a product (globalization). And China and India are trying to change the product now because of ideology and beliefs. But, Japan is in a different position. It has bought the product for decades. It has supported it and developed through it. And, now, all of a sudden, it no longer wants it. What happens when a company's biggest customer suddenly stops buying? There is a crisis. That is the magnitude of what is taking place with Japan. One of the biggest subscribers to globalization is now leaping into the vertical world. And as this happens, it is creating a crisis for the architects of globalization. How should they continue selling their design if those who have been most loyal to it are now jumping ship? And, equally important, if the architects cannot keep Japan in their corner, after decades of investment and support, how do they plan to win over anyone else?

In the vertical world, Japan is no longer operating under the shadows of other nations. It is no longer muted, subdued, or pacified. The limitations that Japan has operated under are being lifted.

Now, the true voice and spirit of Japan will be heard.

CHAPTER EIGHT

The Israeli North Star

Since its inception, Israel has been acting vertically. In many ways, it had no choice. Because of its history and geography, Israel's survival has always been under attack. To develop, Israel could not turn to globalization, that is, integrate its economy or become reliant on its neighbors. There was nobody to integrate with and nobody to rely on. The only path for Israel was to act independently, without the rest of the world, except the US.

This took place on two fronts. The first front was, of course, building a large, strong, and sophisticated military. But, the second, less discussed front, was to create locally-built industries and ecosystems. The government in Tel Aviv knew that ultimately, Israel's success depended on an advanced, self-reliant, and diversified economy. This means that over the past decades, Israel has been building its economy and society with barriers. Some of these barriers were imposed on Israel, while others, Israel established to protect itself.

The "fruit" of those actions turned out to be technology. Technology has allowed Israel to rise and become a leader in the vertical world. Over decades, through vertical thinking, Israel has developed technologies to solve many challenges, like freshwater shortages, with little outside help. These are the types of challenges that much of the world is "reliant" on the global systems to solve. In other words, by acting vertically from the beginning, Israel is able to take independent steps today on a range of issues in a way most nations cannot. Alongside this, Israel has begun offering its technology to governments worldwide, allowing them to take vertical steps as well.

For Israel, the vertical world became a reality because of circumstance. Unlike many other nations, who were only worried about economic growth or development, Israel was more concerned about survival. Now, however, the vertical world is a choice. Nothing is stopping Israel from becoming "globalized" and bringing down barriers. Except, this is not something Israel is pursuing. Presented with two options (globalization or the vertical world), Israel is comfortable with staying vertical. And, if Israel, a nation whose very existence has been challenged and questioned for decades, is doubling down on the vertical world, then the "pull" that globalization once had is indeed diminishing.

From Water To Crops, Israel Goes At It Alone

In 2020, as the world watched the US and China clash over technology, Beijing made a provocative statement: it wanted to achieve self-sufficiency in technology. In other words, China did not want to depend on the US or Europe for things like semiconductors or servers. Except, while China wanted to become self-sufficient, Israel had already achieved this in certain areas.

For example, look at freshwater. Because of Israel's geography, Israel has suffered chronic freshwater shortages for decades. Between 2009 to 2014, Israel - and the Middle East - experienced one of its driest periods in almost 100 years.[181] In fact, in 2001, Israel had to stop using water for agriculture, which was consuming 70% of Israel's water resources at the time.[182] In other words, Israel's water situation was so dire at the beginning of the 21st century that the country had to pick between producing food or giving its people water! Now, thanks to desalination technology, the situation has improved dramatically over the years. Desalination is a process whereby seawater is made drinkable by removing salts and other minerals. Israel has used desalination facilities since the 1970s. [183] But, only recently, as Israel constructed dozens of these facilities across the country, had Israel's water challenges been solved. Starting in mid-2020, Israel began work on a seventh desalination facility on the Mediterranean Sea. Once built, desalination facilities are expected to provide 90% of all water used by Israel's residential and industrial areas.[184] And, in November 2019, Israel's energy minister said that 100% of Israel's tap water would come from desalination in the coming years.[185]

Instead of depending on the world to solve its freshwater challenge, Israel acted independently with technology. Instead of importing water from abroad or becoming dependent on the regional water infrastructure, Israel used technology to become "water independent." This is "vertical action." And, now, the desalination facilities act as a new "barrier" that shelter Israel from the rest of the world's water troubles. But, equally importantly, the desalination technology allows Israel to take vertical steps on a separate front: climate change. One of the effects of climate change is droughts and freshwater shortages. Without desalination, Israel would have relied on the whole world to solve climate problems and procure water. However, with desalination technology, Israel does not depend on climate accords that address global warming. What the rest of the world does on climate is less relevant to Israel as it can solve droughts and freshwater shortages on its own - without anyone else - using technology.

Israel's ability to deal with climate change vertically extends beyond freshwater. In July 2020, Beewise Technologies, an Israeli firm, demonstrated the use of

AI-based robotic bees. The goal was to create "robotic hives" that could offset the death rate of bees as they are needed for pollinating 75% of food crops.[186] Separately, in January 2019, biotechnology students from the Israeli Institute of Technology (Technion) developed a falafel made up of algae called "Algafalafel." Their goal was to invent a source of cheap, nutritious, and widely available protein for the world as the global population grows.[187] Again, Israel is solving an immediate challenge, food production decline related to climate change, by using technology developed locally and not depending on anybody else.

Could Israel enable other nations to act vertically on climate change? Already, Israel is offering its desalination technology to India, a country facing massive water shortages. Suppose India can use Israeli desalination technology to solve its water woes. In that case, New Delhi will also reduce its dependency on the rest of the world when it comes to climate change.

Like with water, Israel is also building self-sufficiency in areas like healthcare and agriculture. In August 2018, Israeli biotech firm "BTG" announced it had developed a brand new fertility treatment that manipulates human cells to increase chances of pregnancy.[188] In August 2020, Kadimastem, another biotech firm in Israel, shared its results treating ALS, a type of neurological disorder. Through its drug, the speed at which ALS spread was reduced by 50%.[189] Israel is also making progress in repairing bone loss (using grafts developed from a patient's fat cells)[190], developing drugs for AIDS that destroy HIV-infected cells[191] , and even creating a cure for cancer.[192] These advances show that Israel is expanding its healthcare system using mostly homegrown technologies. A driver of global connectivity, healthcare (and medical tourism), is now becoming vertical as nations like Israel use technology to build advanced healthcare systems from the ground up.

The situation is not much different when looking at agriculture. In January 2020, two Israeli companies - Cann10 and Epigenetics - announced a new cannabis company. Using biotechnology and epigenetics (allowing genes hidden in the DNA to develop), the two firms seek to create a new strain of cannabis that is easier to grow. The company tested its technology in tomatoes and corn and increased photosynthesis (how plants absorb and convert sunlight to fuel growth) by 100 points. It massively boosted the yield.[193]

These advances are vertical steps towards making Israel "food independent" just as it is water independent. In other words, technology is making Israel self-sufficient in the most critical areas (water, food, and healthcare).

Israel Builds The New Global Fault Lines

The technologies that Israel has developed through vertical thinking are giving rise to a new Israeli design for the world. Instead of using the existing systems, built on the back of globalization, Israel is offering its own alternatives to nations. In October 2020, Gadfin, an Israeli drone company, announced global drone transportation networks. These networks, focused on delivering healthcare, would connect clinics and hospitals worldwide with drones that can supply goods. The next healthcare grids that nations use are being built by a single country (Israel) instead of a cohort of governments or even global institutions. The infrastructure and technology are being supplied, in large part, by Israel and partners that Israel allows (or denies).

Alongside drones, Israel is supplying technology in a way that could lead to the dominance of the US dollar being challenged. In February 2018, the Marshall

Islands, located in the Pacific Ocean, announced a digital currency called "Sovereign," or SOV. And, by doing this, the Marshall Islands would stop using the US dollar.[194] However, what is most shocking, is that the nation helping the Marshall Islands achieve this is Israel. Neema, an Israeli fintech startup, is the main partner working with the Marshall Islands to replace USD with SOV.[195] Nations are tapping Israel to help them break free of globalization and regain sovereignty by developing their own digital currencies. Except, there is another way to look at what Israel is doing in the Marshall Islands. Israel is helping nations challenge the USD. Or, put differently, Israel is assisting governments to become free of Israel's closest ally: the US.

And, this is not just taking place when it comes to currency. In February 2021, Israel tested a drone that uses AI to navigate without GPS.[196] Israel's technology is now challenging the US navigation systems that the world uses. As Israel supplies these AI drones to the world, the parts of the world that are GPS-driven will start to crack. While such actions may have been expected from the US adversaries, it was not expected from the closest allies, like Israel. And, ironically, Israel is not challenging GPS intentionally. It is that as technology advances, traditional systems like GPS are no longer as required.

There is also a significant push by Israel to reimagine how militaries deal with new threats. In June 2020, the Israeli military announced a new mapping software that uses augmented reality and AI. It is similar to Google Street View. Israeli military officers can scan areas in real-time and identify targets using crowds of people to hide within. AI crunches real-time data feeds at the backend to provide officers with insight into what a target may do next (behavior prediction). [197] Such a system represents a new export: intelligence-agency-as-a-service. For many nations in Asia and Africa, who are still building their intelligence capabilities, the Israeli software will supercharge their operations. As this happens, it reduces the reliance these nations have on the other established intelligence agencies (i.e., training, partnerships). Even if Israel's software still depends on intelligence supplied by the established agencies (i.e., CIA, MI6), Israel is now the gatekeeper on what intelligence other nations who buy Israel's software will see.

Instead of "intelligence" being a regional or global activity, Israel can define and control intelligence through its mapping software. The incentives that nations once had to cooperate on intelligence may disappear as the advanced software creates a vertical split in intelligence collection and sharing. Will Israel create its own Five Eyes (a grouping of Anglo-Saxon nations with which the US shares intelligence)? Or will the next flashpoint between Israel and another country be around biases that Israel has inputted into its intelligence AI software?

Vertical Industries, Designed In Tel Aviv

As Israel builds the next generation industries, its journey into the vertical world is accelerating. Take AI-based chips. These are chips designed for AI-based applications, like cloud computing services. And, as nations compete to become AI powers, these chips are becoming more critical than ever before. Countries with these chips, either through manufacturing or access to them, can build powerful AI capabilities. And, those without them will struggle to compete in the New Algorithmic Age (the age of robotics and AI).

When it comes to AI-based chips, Israel is a global leader. In July 2020, a team of students from Israel's Bar-

Ilan University was recognized as one of the top three teams at a competition in Switzerland. The Israeli team developed a new kind of "on-chip" memory, a memory critical for AI.[198] A year earlier, in June 2019, Habana Labs, an Israeli chip startup, announced it had developed the world's fastest AI-based chip that could offer three times more performance than chips currently being used in data centers around the world. [199] Israel is also becoming a hub for foreign companies to develop AI-based chips. In August 2019, Intel announced its first AI-based chip, designed in Israel. [200] At the same time, Nvidia has built an AI-research center in Israel [201]. Similarly, Hangzhou Wahaha Group, one of the largest companies in China, has established an AI-research center at the University of Haifa.[202]

As Israel builds AI-based chips for the world, it will challenge globalization. At one level, Israel will give the world new options for chips. The world will no longer only rely on the US, China, Taiwan, South Korea, or Japan. At another level, Israel's chips could force the government in Tel Aviv to take radical steps. For example, Israel may begin limiting or blocking out investment from certain nations to protect its technology. Such decisions would represent new walls based on technology. Or, other governments may become concerned that Israel is gaining a monopoly over AI-based chips. These governments could manufacture products that do not operate with Israeli chips. The next manufacturing processes could be vertical. They might exclude specific hardware or software because of where they originate from. There is also another level where Israel decides to discard the US (and Western Europe) model and supply its chip technology to the world.

Unlike the traditional chip powers, who never shared the designs or critical know-how with the world, Israel may use chips to build its footprint in other nations. It could begin offering countries the ability to develop their own "chip industries" from scratch. Just as Israel may export intelligence-agency-as-a-service, it may also export "chips-manufacturing-as-a-service."

A similar, vertical reality is emerging with self-driving cars. In April 2019, Cortica, an Israeli startup, announced that it had developed new AI technology to improve how self-driving vehicles can operate. Cortica's technology is being embedded into chips that power autonomous vehicles.[203] At the same time, in March 2017, Mobileye, an Israeli developer of driver assistance and vision technologies, was acquired by Intel. From a global context, Mobileye is considered one of the most advanced self-driving companies in the world.[204] Just as with AI-based chips, Israel is building leadership in self-driving vehicles. Unlike the US, Germany, Japan, or South Korea, which are manufacturing the physical vehicles and developing the software, Israel is working mainly on the latter. Israel seems to be more focused on the brains of self-driving vehicles than physical vehicles.

The Israeli self-driving brains represent a new vector in the world. The whole world will want them, but Israel could play favorites, only exporting the brains to specific nations. In other words, Israel could build limits on who can use Israeli technology and who cannot. Alternatively, some countries may be uncomfortable using Israeli brains in self-driving cars. And, they may outright ban it because of cultural or historical feelings. In these cases, governments would be erecting new barriers to block out Israeli technology. But, there is also the geopolitical way these brains could give rise to the vertical world. The brains may be used by other nations trying to achieve a certain level of technological advancement, so they are not reliant on the rest of the world.

This is already happening. In February 2020, Shaanxi Heavy Duty Automobile, a Chinese truck manufacturer, signed a deal with Innoviz Technologies, an Israeli sensor company, to develop 600 self-driving trucks for a Chinese port.[205] While today China depends on the US for cutting edge self-driving technology, it may soon develop its local capabilities. And the stepping stone that allows China to "unplug" from the US may be the Israeli brains. China could use Israel's technology to develop its self-driving capabilities to a point where it no longer needs US companies or talent. And, the US might be waking up to this threat. In December 2020, the US warned that Chinese investments in Israeli technology presented challenges to national security.[206] Before this, in August 2020, the US and Israel discussed how to ensure Israel did not use Chinese technology in its 5G network.[207] For the US, it is becoming clear that China is using Israeli technology to circumvent US sanctions - and eventually challenge the US-led world order.

In other words, the vertical world is not just about actions that one nation is taking against another through technology. It is also about how these actions may end up redefining pre-exiting and new relationships as well.

Conclusion

For decades, Israel lived in an atmosphere of disbelief. A prime example of this is India. While today the Israel-India relationship continues to reach new heights, it was a very different story in the not too distant past. Many passports issued by the Indian government had a statement warning that the passport was not valid for South Africa or Israel. It was India's way of saying it did not recognize these nations and their sovereignty. This is the reality, of having its existence denied, that Israel has been forced to develop and rise under. Ideas of globalization, like integrating with other nations, were unthinkable for Israel if it were to survive and prosper.

Yet, Israel pushed forward. And, as it did this, it used technology in incredible ways. It is no coincidence that Israel's development as a nation and Israel's technological advances took place along the same timelines. They went hand-in-hand and fed off each other. As this happened, Israel was able to reinforce its borders and position in the world. The more Israel could safeguard critical areas, like freshwater, the more its existence in the region was secured.

Now, Israel's vertical steps are being seen differently. Governments are waking up to the fact that Israel does not need the world the same way other countries do. On critical issues, like climate change and defense, Israel is using technology to solve problems on its own. And, from this attitude, Israel is also giving rise to new industries that are allowing it to act even more vertically. How does globalization convince Israel to join it? In short, it cannot. Based on the steps Israel has taken, Israel is already sold on the vertical world.

The next phase for Israel now depends on how it uses its technology on the world stage. Until now, Israel has helped itself. Going forward, Israel will offer its technologies, selectively or not, to empower other nations. This will further accelerate the vertical world. Governments will either use Israeli technology to solve problems that they once depended on the world to solve. Or they will shun Israeli technology completely. As the vertical world takes shape, Israel's technology may represent a new division in the world. Some nations may want it. Others may not. Regardless, Israeli technology may push countries to choose a side, accelerating the push away from globalization and uniform thinking even more.

CONCLUSION

The New Global Design

A few decades ago, scientists came out with a dire prediction. In 5.5 billion years, the Earth will be destroyed. The Sun will heat up, expand, and "burn" the Earth. All life, including the human species, will cease to exist. When this prediction came out, all kinds of questions emerged. What would happen to humanity? Should steps be taken now, or should this be left to future generations? Is there a way to keep the Sun from exploding? Except, these questions, while essential and existential, were still surface deep. They did not reflect the actual "transformation" that would take place in the future. In a few billion years, a "design" that the world depends on is predicted to fail. Everything connected to this failing design is going to be affected in unimaginable ways. The world's foundation will collapse, and everything standing on it, from global food production to the global climate to the survival of species, will collapse as well.

This is analogous to globalization. In the face of technology, the design that underpins the world, that powers nations, businesses, societies, and economies, is starting to collapse. Unlike the explosion of the Sun, which will take place in the future, the current model of globalization is losing steam today. The shift away from globalization is already underway as technology challenges global systems and ideas. However, unlike with the Sun collapsing, where nobody knows what will happen next, with globalization, there is clarity of what will follow: the world becoming vertical.

The severity and gravitas are the same. The vertical world is about nations reclaiming sovereignty through technology. Instead of being tied to the old model of globalization, because there has been no other choice, governments are using technology to reimagine their destiny and place in the world. Instead of integrating deeper with each other, nations are establishing walls and barriers using technology. The idea that the world can operate in a uniform, singular way is gone. Now, because of technology, the world is becoming sporadic, chaotic, and volatile, as nations move in all kinds of directions, many of which counter one another. And, businesses are being pushed and pulled, testing their global strategies, profitability, and business models like never before.

The vertical world is here. There is no going back to the way things were. Like an abstract painting, people will interpret the vertical world differently. That is because, in many ways, the vertical world is a paradox as much as it is a paradigm. It represents many things at the same time. And, sometimes, these things can appear to contradict one another. At one moment, Japan is bringing the vertical world to life by encouraging robot-driven manufacturing. And, yet, at another moment, South Korea is bringing the vertical world to life by discouraging robot-driven manufacturing. How can these both be possible? Because the vertical world is being formed by nations, who are approaching the same technologies from different angles. And, in some cases, countries are approaching the same issue differently based on the situation. At one moment, India wants to manage data through its sovereign laws, and yet, at another moment, India wants to manage data through global data rules. There is no consistency in the vertical world. Instead of nations standing by a policy or position for years, they are constantly changing positions based on what is at stake. This results in countries making decisions that diverge from what was done in the past or expected.

The vertical world is fluid. It is ever-changing. And this can cloud what is happening for those who look at the vertical world through a black and white lens. The actual colors of the vertical world cannot be seen by reducing what is taking place to a fight between the US and China or nations exiting the Americanized world. These are only by-products of the vertical world. Instead, those who seek to understand the vertical world, and succeed in it, must view this new era as a "period of radical transformation" whereby every system, approach, and idea that the world is built on is morphing into something different. And, at the core of this transformation, technology is weakening the threads that have woven the nations of the world together for decades.

It is also important to view technology companies as new stakeholders in the vertical world. In the new vertical design of the world, these companies are equal to governments. One example is Facebook. When it announced "Libra," a digital currency, in June 2019, governments and central banks were up in arms, rejecting the notion that a technology company should control a currency that billions of people may use. Facebook returned to the drawing board, redesigning the currency to conform with the global rules. Facebook was willing to do this. The next technology company might not be. The services that technology firms like Facebook are developing will upend the established order as these companies gain more power over how the world works.

For those seeking leadership in the vertical world, the following realities must be accepted as the new status quo. First, new "technology borders" are emerging all over the world. These borders are crisscrossing, not just dividing nations on the world stage but also dividing nations internally. These borders form based on how governments approach technology (i.e., data monopolies, AI-based platforms). And, they are also forming based on whose technology a nation uses (i.e., US, Chinese, Russian, or homegrown). In some ways, these technology borders represent a new kind of "Iron Curtain" that threatens to divide and split the world along new lines.

Second, the way people and ideas move throughout the world is undergoing a massive change. Instead of the world being accessible to everyone, it is fast becoming restricted and walled off to specific people. As technology drives economies and business models, governments are becoming fearful about who they are letting in (and have let in). Are "foreigners" going to support the nation they live in or the nation they (or their parents) came from? This paranoia is forcing governments to rethink their immigration strategy. In the West, this goes beyond just changing who can enter. It is about redesigning the very "ethos" of Western society. Ideals like opportunity, equality, and accessibility, are now being redefined in the vertical world.

Third, and lastly, the vertical world means the current form of globalization is ending. An era of rebirth is underway as the established norms, protocols, and ideals are discarded. The current design is being upended. But, this does not mean that globalization itself is disappearing. This would not be possible. As the current form of globalization ends, "next globalization" is also beginning. And, next globalization stands like a pink plant in a garden of green trees. It is significantly different from what has existed before. In next globalization, the world will not be integrated on the same axis. Next globalization will revolve around multiple streams of integration, led by different nations (and businesses) who oppose one another. The very definition of globalization will change as barriers and restrictions become an accepted norm. At the same time, unlike the old version of globalization, which focused entirely on the "global systems," next globalization is also focused on the inner workings of nations. Instead of trickle-down, it will also be trickle-up.

The vertical world is not a temporary phenomenon or a fad. It will not disappear in a decade, nor will it dissipate if one superpower trumps another. Like a planet forming from molten lava and rock, the vertical world is the new global geography that will only become more permanent as time passes. There is no escaping it. And, there is no ignoring it. Right now, the vertical world is only being driven by less than ten nations. And, already, the world is splitting. In the coming years, dozens more countries will jump into the vertical world. And, dozens more technology companies will emerge as global forces. When a hundred stakeholders are thinking vertically, the world will be transformed on an unimaginable scale.

The strategy of businesses and governments must change fast. Governments will not be able to stand by the prescriptions of the past, nor will companies be able to recycle old strategies. Capitals and corporate board rooms will be pressed to develop new solutions in faster and faster cycles, to address the challenges (and opportunities) the vertical world is bringing.

While modern-day globalization was conceived during a meeting in August 1941, it took decades of negotiations and implementation for the world to become globalized. This is not the path the vertical world is taking. No consensus or deliberation is causing the vertical world to form. Nor are there decades of negotiations needed to bring the vertical world into reality. The vertical world is beginning because nations are fed up with the existing model. And, it is forming at a speed where months are the new decades. The power and potential that globalization promised nations and businesses are now being offered by the vertical world.

Like Shangri-La, the vertical world holds countless riches and opportunities. But getting there is the tricky part. The path is riddled with chaos and temptation. But, those who venture out, who brave the obstacles in their way, will view the vertical world as their salvation. On the other hand, those who fear the vertical world, or worse, suppress its rise, will find themselves confined to a dangerous future, where everybody is viewed as an enemy, and every global transformation is considered to be a threat. The only way to navigate uncertainty is to pick a direction and move. The vertical world presents two paths. The destiny of countries, companies, and cities hangs in the balance.

References

Chapter One: The New Borders of Europe

[i] Gold, Hadas. "UK Bans Huawei from Its 5G Network in Rapid About-face." CNN. July 14, 2020. https://www.cnn.com/2020/07/14/tech/huawei-uk-ban/index.html.

[ii] "UK to Exclude Chinese Students from Sensitive Subjects - Times." Reuters. October 01, 2020. https://ca.reuters.com/article/idUSKBN26M5YY.

[iii] Presse, AFP - Agence France. "UK Launches Bill To Stop 'Malicious' Foreign Takeovers." UK Launches Bill To Stop 'Malicious' Foreign Takeovers. November 11, 2020. https://www.barrons.com/news/uk-launches-bill-to-stop-malicious-foreign-takeovers-01605087607.

[iv] "Iran Signs $16bn Deal to Buy 80 Boeing Aircraft." BBC News. December 11, 2016. https://www.bbc.com/news/business-38280724.

[v] Tung, Liam. "Meet GAIA-X: This Is Europe's Bid to Get Cloud Independence from US and China Giants." ZDNet. June 08, 2020. https://www.zdnet.com/article/meet-gaia-x-this-is-europes-bid-to-get-cloud-independence-from-us-and-china-giants/.

[vi] *Promoting Public Safety, Privacy, and the Rule of Law Around the World: The Purpose and Impact of the CLOUD Act.* PDF. Washington, DC: US Department of Justice, April 2019.

[vii] Anderson, Tim. "German Ministry Hellbent on Taking Back Control of 'digital Sovereignty', Cutting Dependency on Microsoft." The Register® - Biting the Hand That Feeds IT. September 19, 2019. https://www.theregister.com/2019/09/19/german_government_report_digital_sovereignty/.

[viii] Sample, Ian. "Scientists Plan Huge European AI Hub to Compete with US." The Guardian. April 23, 2018. https://www.theguardian.com/science/2018/apr/23/scientists-plan-huge-european-ai-hub-to-compete-with-us.

[ix] Johnson, Khari. "ELLIS Launches $220 Million Initiative to Keep AI Talent in Europe." VentureBeat. December 11, 2019. https://venturebeat.com/2019/12/10/ellis-launches-220-million-initiative-to-keep-ai-talent-in-europe/.

[x] Lomas, Natasha. "Google Fined $2.7BN for EU Antitrust Violations over Shopping Searches." TechCrunch. June 27, 2017. https://techcrunch.com/2017/06/27/google-fined-e2-42bn-for-eu-antitrust-violations-over-shopping-searches/.

[xi] Schulze, Elizabeth. "If You Want to Know What a US Tech Crackdown May Look Like, Check out What Europe Did." CNBC. June 07, 2019. https://www.cnbc.com/2019/06/07/how-google-facebook-amazon-and-apple-faced-eu-tech-antitrust-rules.html.

[xii] Kharpal, Arjun. "Facebook Fined $122 Million by EU for Giving 'misleading Information' about Its Takeover of WhatsApp." CNBC. May 18, 2017. https://www.cnbc.com/2017/05/18/facebook-fine-eu-whatsapp-takeover.html.

[xiii] Perper, Rosie. "Facebook Could Be Fined up to $1.63 Billion for a Massive Breach That May Have Violated EU Privacy Laws." Business Insider. September 30, 2018. https://www.businessinsider.com/facebook-eu-fine-163-billion-massive-data-breach-50-million-users-2018-10.

[xiv] Chee, Foo Yun. "Facebook Sues EU Antitrust Regulator for Excessive Data Requests." Reuters. July 27, 2020. https://www.reuters.com/article/us-eu-facebook-antitrust-idUSKCN24S2BN.

[xv] Porter, Jon. "EU Antitrust Regulators Have Facebook's Libra Currency in Their Sights." The Verge. August 21, 2019.

https://www.theverge.com/2019/8/21/20826290/facebook-libra-digital-currency-european-union-commission-regulators-antitrust-competition.

[xvi] Lomas, Natasha. "EU Digs in on Digital Tax Plan, after US Quits Talks." TechCrunch. June 18, 2020. https://techcrunch.com/2020/06/18/eu-digs-in-on-digital-tax-plan-after-us-quits-talks/.

[xvii] Lomas, Natasha. "Europe Will Go It Alone on Digital Tax Reform in 2021 If It Must, Says EU President, as Bloc Directs €150BN in COVID-19 Relief toward Cloud, AI and Broadband." TechCrunch. September 16, 2020. https://techcrunch.com/2020/09/16/europe-will-go-it-alone-on-digital-tax-reform-in-2021-if-it-must-says-eu-president-as-bloc-directs-e150bn-in-covid-19-relief-toward-cloud-ai-and-broadband/.

[xviii] Hanbury, Mary. "Amazon Is about to Be Clobbered with a Big New Tax, and Its First Instinct Is to Slam 3rd-party Sellers with Higher Costs." Business Insider. August 20, 2019. https://www.businessinsider.com/amazon-passes-french-digital-services-tax-onto-third-party-sellers-2019-8.

[xix] "Macron, Trump Agree to Hold off on Digital Tax for Tech Giants: DW: 20.01.2020." DW.COM. January 20,

2020. https://www.dw.com/en/macron-trump-agree-to-hold-off-on-digital-tax-for-tech-giants/a-52079172.

[xx] Daley, Jason. "Europe Applies Strict Regulations to CRISPR Crops." Smithsonian.com. July 27, 2018. https://www.smithsonianmag.com/smart-news/europe-applies-strict-regulations-gene-edited-crops-180969774/.

[xxi] "Dutch Farm Minister Opens Door to Gene-editing Crops." DutchNews.nl. October 31, 2018. https://www.dutchnews.nl/news/2018/10/dutch-farm-minister-opens-door-to-gene-editing-crops/.

[xxii] Knolle, Kirsti. "Austria Calls for European Stance on Huawei to Ensure Competition." Reuters. February 13, 2019. https://in.reuters.com/article/us-huawei-europe-austria/austria-calls-for-european-stance-on-huawei-to-ensure-competition-idINKCN1Q22BO.

[xxiii] "France's Macron Announces Creation of Space Force Command: DW: 13.07.2019." DW.COM. July 13, 2019. https://www.dw.com/en/frances-macron-announces-creation-of-space-force-command/a-49581694.

[xxiv] Posaner, Joshua. "Germany Wary of Macron's Space Force." POLITICO. July 29, 2019. https://www.politico.eu/article/germany-wary-emmanuel-macron-space-force/.

[xxv] Posaner, Joshua. "NATO Plans Space Center to Counter Russia, China Satellite Threats." POLITICO. October 20, 2020. https://www.politico.eu/article/nato-will-launch-space-center-to-counter-russia-china-satellite-threats/.

[xxvi] Teffer, Peter. "Bienkowska Bows Out, with No EU 'Space Force' in Sight." EUobserver. August 2, 2019. https://euobserver.com/foreign/145587.

[xxvii] "A Digital Euro? ECB Assessing Safe Alternatives to Cryptocurrencies." Euronews. April 02, 2021. https://www.euronews.com/2020/10/02/a-digital-euro-european-central-bank-assessing-safe-alternative-to-cryptocurrencies.

[xxviii] hPost, Kollen. "Digital Euro Sees First Successful Test at the Bank of France." Cointelegraph. May 20, 2020. https://cointelegraph.com/news/digital-euro-sees-first-successful-test-at-the-bank-of-france.

[xxix] Shome, Arnab. "Poland Is Developing National Cryptocurrency: Finance Magnates." Finance Magnates | Financial and Business News. January 17, 2018. https://www.financemagnates.com/cryptocurrency/news/poland-developing-national-cryptocurrency/.

[xxx] Hashim, Husayn. "Estonian Central Bank to Conduct Digital Currency Research." Cointelegraph. October 03, 2020. https://cointelegraph.com/news/estonian-central-bank-to-conduct-digital-currency-research.

Chapter Two: A Divided Middle East

[xxxi] England, Andrew, and Simeon Kerr. "Saudi Arabia Tries to Lure Multinationals from Dubai." Financial Times. January 10, 2021. https://www.ft.com/content/b968a082-486b-4eb0-b268-e1f2377891d9.

[xxxii] "UAE Government Launches 'Moonshot 2071' Programme." Khaleej Times. February 2, 2021. https://www.khaleejtimes.com/business/local/uae-government-launches-moonshot-2071-programme.

[xxxiii] "UAE Plans Unmanned Mission to Mars by 2021." Middle East News | Al Jazeera. July 16, 2014. https://www.aljazeera.com/news/2014/7/16/uae-plans-unmanned-mission-to-mars-by-2021.

[xxxiv] Yeung, Jessie. "The UAE Has Successfully Launched the Arab World's First Mars Mission, as This Summer's Space Race Heats up." CNN. November 24, 2020.

https://www.cnn.com/2020/07/19/middleeast/uae-mars-hope-launch-intl-hnk-scn-scli/index.html.

[xxxv] "Saudi Arabia Establishes Space Agency In Leadership Shakeup." SpaceWatch.Global. December 30, 2018. https://spacewatch.global/2018/12/saudi-arabia-establishes-space-agency-in-leadership-shakeup/.

[xxxvi] Rashad, Marwa. "Saudi Arabia Plans $2 Billion Boost for Space Programme by 2030." Reuters. October 28, 2020. https://www.reuters.com/article/us-saudi-economy-space-idUSKBN27D1ZH.

[xxxvii] Godinho, Varun. "UAE Prepares to Launch Navigation Satellite in 2021." Gulf Business. August 10, 2020. https://gulfbusiness.com/uae-prepares-to-launch-navigation-satellite-in-2021/.

[xxxviii] "Israeli and Emirati Firms Sign 'historic Agreement' to Jointly Combat COVID-19." The Times of Israel. July 03, 2020. https://www.timesofisrael.com/israeli-and-emirati-firms-sign-historic-agreement-to-jointly-combat-covid-19/.

[xxxix] "Netanyahu Met MBS, Pompeo in Saudi Arabia: Israeli Media." Al Jazeera. November 23, 2020. https://www.aljazeera.com/news/2020/11/23/netanyahu-met-with-mbs-pompeo-in-saudi-arabia-israeli-sources.

[xl] "Abu Dhabi Police to Set up Police Centre on Mars." Khaleej Times. November 16, 2017. https://www.khaleejtimes.com/nation/abu-dhabi//abu-dhabi-police-to-set-up-police-centre-on-mars.

[xli] "Cloning a Punishable Offense." Arab News. April 13, 2015. https://www.arabnews.com/saudi-arabia/news/731846.

[xlii] "UAE and Saudi Arabia Work on Cross-border Digital Currency Plan." The National. December 13, 2017. https://www.thenationalnews.com/business/technology/uae-and-saudi-arabia-work-on-cross-border-digital-currency-plan-1.684176.

[xliii] Moon, Mariella. "Saudi Arabia and UAE Test Cryptocurrency for Cross-border Payments." Engadget. February 04, 2019. https://www.engadget.com/2019-02-03-saudi-uae-cryptocurrency.html.

[xliv] Ulmer, Alexandra, and Deisy Buitrago. "Enter the 'petro': Venezuela to Launch Oil-backed Cryptocurrency." Reuters. December 03, 2017. https://www.reuters.com/article/us-venezuela-economy-idUSKBN1DX0SQ.

[xlv] Anand, Nupur. "India Must Decide If It Hates Cryptocurrencies More than a Good Oil Deal." Quartz.

May 02, 2018. https://qz.com/india/1267691/venezuela-woos-india-with-30-discount-on-crude-oil-if-paid-in-its-cryptocurrency-petro/.

[xlvi] Chan, Minnie. "Chinese Drone Factory in Saudi Arabia First in Middle East." South China Morning Post. March 26, 2017. https://www.scmp.com/news/china/diplomacy-defence/article/2081869/chinese-drone-factory-saudi-arabia-first-middle-east.

[xlvii] Tucker, Patrick. "SecDef: China Is Exporting Killer Robots to the Mideast." Defense One. November 05, 2019. https://www.defenseone.com/technology/2019/11/secdef-china-exporting-killer-robots-mideast/161100/.

[xlviii] Helou, Agnes. "Saudi Arabia Is Developing a New Counter-drone System." Defense News. January 08, 2020. https://www.defensenews.com/unmanned/2020/01/08/saudi-arabia-is-developing-a-new-counter-drone-system/.

[xlix] Oweis, Khaled Yacoub. "Saudi Arabia Will Make Drones next Year Says Military." The National. April 29, 2020. https://www.thenationalnews.com/world/saudi-arabia-will-make-drones-next-year-says-military-1.1012269.

Chapter Three: India Fights Against Next Colonialism

[50] Agrawal, Rajat. "Why India Rejected Facebook's 'free' Version of the Internet." Mashable. February 09, 2016. https://mashable.com/2016/02/09/why-facebook-free-basics-failed-india/.

[51] Punit, Itika Sharma. "Amazon and Flipkart Are Speechless after India Announces New Foreign Investment Rules." Quartz. March 29, 2016. https://qz.com/india/649873/amazon-and-flipkart-are-speechless-after-india-announces-new-foreign-investment-rules/.

[52] Russell, Jon. "New E-commerce Restrictions in India Just Ruined Christmas for Amazon and Walmart." TechCrunch. December 27, 2018. https://techcrunch.com/2018/12/27/amazon-walmart-india-e-commerce-restrictions/.

[53] Vincent, James. "Amazon and Walmart Hit Hard after New E-commerce Rules in India Restrict Sales." The Verge. February 01, 2019. https://www.theverge.com/2019/2/1/18206538/amazon-walmart-flipkart-india-e-commerce-rules-regulation-chaos.

[54] Betigeri, Aarti. "India's Demographic Timebomb." Lowy Institute. July 18, 2018. https://www.lowyinstitute.org/the-interpreter/indias-demographic-timebomb.

[55] Hamel, Kristofer. "Look East Instead of West for the Future Global Middle Class." OECD Development Matters. May 07, 2019. https://oecd-development-matters.org/2019/05/07/look-east-instead-of-west-for-the-future-global-middle-class/.

[56] "Giant Leap: 'India to Have over 500 Million Smartphone Users By 2022'." The Financial Express. October 24, 2018. https://www.financialexpress.com/industry/technology/giant-leap-india-to-have-over-500-million-smartphone-users-by-2022/1358972/.

[57] "Apple to Open Its First Store in India next Year." The Economic Times. February 27, 2020. https://economictimes.indiatimes.com/tech/hardware/apple-to-open-its-first-store-in-india-next-year/articleshow/74329158.cms?from=mdr.

[58] KS, Bavadharini. "All You Wanted to Know about Data Localisation." The Hindu BusinessLine. October 29, 2018. https://www.thehindubusinessline.com/opinion/columns/slate/all-you-wanted-to-know-about-data-localisation/article25363062.ece.

[59] Basu, Arindrajit, and Justin Sherman. "Key Global Takeaways From India's Revised Personal Data Protection

Bill." Lawfare. January 23, 2020. https://www.lawfareblog.com/key-global-takeaways-indias-revised-personal-data-protection-bill.

[60] Singh, Manish. "India Restricts American Express from Adding New Customers for Violating Data Storage Rules." TechCrunch. April 23, 2021. https://techcrunch.com/2021/04/23/india-restricts-american-express-from-adding-new-customers-for-violating-data-storage-rules/.

[61] Sharma, Yogima Seth, and Surabhi Agarwal. "Artificial Intelligence: Niti Aayog to Come out with National Policy on Artificial Intelligence Soon." The Economic Times. March 21, 2018. https://economictimes.indiatimes.com/news/economy/policy/niti-aayog-to-come-out-with-national-policy-on-artificial-intelligence-soon/articleshow/63387764.cms.

[62] Sharma, Yogima. "Niti Aayog Bats for Ending Data Monopoly." The Economic Times. May 17, 2019. https://economictimes.indiatimes.com/news/economy/policy/niti-aayog-bats-for-ending-data-monopoly/articleshow/69364496.cms.

[63] Sharma, Yogima Seth. "NITI Aayog Invites Bids for National Data Platform." The Economic Times. July 19,

2019.

https://economictimes.indiatimes.com/tech/internet/niti-aayog-invites-bids-for-national-data-platform/articleshow/70291168.cms?from=mdr.

[64] Rai, Saritha. "Amazon, Google Face Tough Rules in India's E-Commerce Draft." BloombergQuint. July 04, 2020. https://www.bloombergquint.com/business/amazon-google-face-tough-rules-in-india-s-e-commerce-draft.

[65] Dasgupta, Neha, and Aditya Kalra. "Exclusive: U.S. Tells India It Is Mulling Caps on H-1B Visas to Deter Data Rules - Sources." Reuters. June 19, 2019. https://www.reuters.com/article/us-usa-trade-india-exclusive-idUSKCN1TK2LG.

[66] "India's Digital Sky Drones Platform Goes Live For Startups, Drone-Makers." Inc42 Media. August 18, 2020. https://inc42.com/buzz/indias-digital-sky-drones-platform-goes-live-for-startups-drone-makers/.

[67] Chiu, Karen. "China's DJI Drones Aren't Cleared for Take-off in India." Abacus | SCMP. August 21, 2020. https://www.scmp.com/abacus/culture/article/3098176/india-opens-more-its-sky-consumer-drones-most-chinas-dji-dont.

[68] Sheth, Hemani. "Indian Intelligence Agencies Flag over 50 Chinese Apps including TikTok: Report." The Hindu BusinessLine. June 20, 2020. https://www.thehindubusinessline.com/info-tech/indian-intelligence-agencies-flag-over-50-chinese-apps-including-tiktok-zoom-report/article31857225.ece.

[69] Singh, Manish. "India Bans TikTok, Dozens of Other Chinese Apps." TechCrunch. June 29, 2020. https://techcrunch.com/2020/06/29/india-bans-tiktok-dozens-of-other-chinese-apps/.

[70] Daws, Ryan. "India Is the Latest Country Preparing to Ban Huawei from Its 5G." Telecoms Tech News. August 14, 2020. https://telecomstechnews.com/news/2020/aug/14/india-latest-country-ban-huawei-5g/.

[71] "India Bans PUBG, Baidu and More than 100 Apps Linked to China." BBC News. September 02, 2020. https://www.bbc.com/news/technology-53998205.

[72] Nandy, Madhurima, and Swaraj Singh Dhanjal. "Alibaba Hits Pause on Its India Investments." Mint. August 27, 2020. https://www.livemint.com/companies/news/alibaba-puts-

fresh-investment-plans-in-india-on-hold-11598459771981.html.

[73] Laghate, Gaurav. "Chinese Smartphone Manufacturer Vivo Pulls out as Title Sponsor of IPL 2020." The Economic Times. August 05, 2020. https://economictimes.indiatimes.com/news/sports/vivo-pulls-out-as-title-sponsor-of-ipl-2020/articleshow/77358587.cms.

[74] "Vivo Back as IPL Title Sponsor for 2021 Season." ESPNcricinfo. February 18, 2021. https://www.espncricinfo.com/story/ipl-2021-vivo-back-as-title-sponsor-1252177.

[75] "India Wants TikTok Parent ByteDance to Deposit $11 Million to Get Access to Frozen Bank Accounts – Media." RT International. April 06, 2021. https://www.rt.com/business/520228-india-bytedance-frozen-accounts/.

[76] "India Blocks China-made Wireless Device Imports: Report." Al Jazeera. May 07, 2021. https://www.aljazeera.com/economy/2021/5/7/india-blocks-china-made-wireless-device-imports-report.

[77] Ruiyao, Luo. "Indian Tech Workers Seek Lifelines as Chinese Firms Exit amid Border Spat." South China

Morning Post. December 27, 2020. https://www.scmp.com/week-asia/politics/article/3115355/indian-tech-workers-seek-lifelines-chinese-firms-exit-amid.

[78] Suneja, Kirtika. "A New E-commerce Policy to Curb Chinese Imports." The Economic Times. June 19, 2020. https://economictimes.indiatimes.com/news/economy/policy/ecomm-products-to-wear-their-origin-on-their-sleeve/articleshow/76452927.cms?from=mdr.

Chapter Four: Raising The Korean Flag

[79] McGoogan, Cara. "South Korea Introduces World's First 'robot Tax'." The Telegraph. August 09, 2017. https://www.telegraph.co.uk/technology/2017/08/09/south-korea-introduces-worlds-first-robot-tax/.

[80] Muir, Paul. "South Korea Mulls 20% Cryptocurrency Tax." Asia Times. February 18, 2020. https://asiatimes.com/2020/01/south-korea-considers-20-crypto-tax/.

[81] Ramirez, Elaine. "Why South Korea Is Banning All Foreigners From Trading Cryptocurrency." Forbes.

January 24, 2018. https://www.forbes.com/sites/elaineramirez/2018/01/23/why-south-korea-is-banning-all-foreigners-from-trading-cryptocurrency/?sh=50b0aa5f7345.

[82] Crichton, Danny. "South Korea Passes One of the World's First Comprehensive Cryptocurrency Laws." TechCrunch. March 05, 2020. https://techcrunch.com/2020/03/05/south-korea-passes-one-of-the-worlds-first-comprehensive-cryptocurrency-laws/.

[83] Min-kyung, Jung. "BOK to Virtually Test Distribution of Digital Currency next Year." The Korea Herald. October 07, 2020. http://m.koreaherald.com/view.php?ud=20201007000809.

[84] Rizzo, Cailey. "Why South Korea Spent $77 Million to Get You to Eat Kimchi." Travel Leisure. August 20, 2016. https://www.travelandleisure.com/food-drink/south-korea-spent-millions-on-kimchi.

[85] Lee, Jungah, and Ian King. "Qualcomm Fined $853 Million by South Korean Antitrust Agency." Bloomberg.com. December 27, 2016. https://www.bloomberg.com/news/articles/2016-12-

28/qualcomm-fined-853-million-by-south-korea-s-antitrust-agency-ix8csvth.

[86] "South Korea Fines Qualcomm $854 Million for Violating Competition Laws." The Economic Times. December 28, 2016. https://economictimes.indiatimes.com/news/international/business/south-korea-fines-qualcomm-854-million-for-violating-competition-laws/articleshow/56217919.cms?from=mdr.

[87] "South Korea to Make 5G and AI Centrepieces of Country's 'New Deal'." South China Morning Post. May 07, 2020. https://www.scmp.com/tech/big-tech/article/3083293/south-korea-make-5g-and-ai-centrepieces-economys-new-deal-post.

[88] "AI Employment Becomes Legally Acceptable for Korean Drug Developers - Pulse by Maeil Business News Korea." Pulse. November 26, 2018. https://pulsenews.co.kr/view.php?year=2018&no=738900.

[89] Temperton, James. "Samsung Developing Robots to Replace Cheap Chinese Labour." WIRED UK. October 19, 2015. https://www.wired.co.uk/article/samsung-south-korea-robots-cheap-labour.

[90] Brian, Matt. "South Korea to Develop New Open-source OS to Rival IOS, Android." The Next Web. August 22, 2011. https://thenextweb.com/news/south-korea-to-develop-new-open-source-os-to-rival-ios-android.

[91] Bunton, Cam. "What Is Samsung's Tizen OS and What Devices Is It On?" Pocket-Lint. March 15, 2021. https://www.pocket-lint.com/phones/news/samsung/127527-what-is-tizen-and-what-devices-will-it-appear-on.

[92] Udin, Efe. "South Korea Sternly Rejects U.S. Pressure to Ban Huawei 5G -." Gizchina.com. October 15, 2020. https://www.gizchina.com/2020/10/15/south-korea-sternly-rejects-u-s-pressure-to-ban-huawei-5g/.

[93] "Huawei Launches 5G Lab in South Korea, but Keeps Event Low-key after US Ban." CNBC. May 29, 2019. https://www.cnbc.com/2019/05/30/huawei-launches-5g-lab-in-south-korea-keeps-it-low-key-after-us-ban.html.

[94] "Huawei Inks Partnership to Support S. Korea's AI Companies." The Korea Herald. June 19, 2020. http://www.koreaherald.com/view.php?ud=20200619000539.

[95] "Samsung Could Manufacture Huawei's 5G Chips in Return for Smartphone Market Share." Gizmochina. June

13, 2020.
https://www.gizmochina.com/2020/06/13/samsung-could-manufacture-huaweis-5g-chips-in-return-for-smartphone-market-share/.

Chapter Five: A Walled Off Russia

[96] "Russia Begins Trials on Voice Control of Military Robots." TASS. June 29, 2020. https://tass.com/defense/1172663.

[97] "Russia Considers 'unplugging' from Internet." BBC News. February 11, 2019. https://www.bbc.com/news/technology-47198426.

[98] Wakefield, Jane. "Russia 'successfully Tests' Its Unplugged Internet." BBC News. December 24, 2019. https://www.bbc.com/news/technology-50902496.

[99] Gambrell, Jon. "Iran Is Making the Internet Halal." The Independent. January 29, 2018. https://www.independent.co.uk/news/world/middle-east/iran-halal-internet-national-information-network-web-freedoms-citizens-access-social-media-telegram-facebook-twitter-instagram-youtube-a8182841.html.

[100] "Iran Rolls out Domestic Internet." BBC News. August 29, 2016. https://www.bbc.com/news/technology-37212456.

[101] Esfandiari, Golnaz. "Iran To Work With China To Create National Internet System." RadioFreeEurope/RadioLiberty. September 04, 2020. https://www.rferl.org/a/iran-china-national-internet-system-censorship/30820857.html.

[102] Shapiro, Daniel, and Natasha Yefimova-Trilling. "Russia Matters." Russian Population Decline in Spotlight Again | Russia Matters. September 13, 2019. https://www.russiamatters.org/blog/russian-population-decline-spotlight-again.

[103] Nikolova, Maria. "Robot Lawyer Set to Replace 3,000 Employees at Sberbank." Finance Feeds. January 03, 2017. https://financefeeds.com/robot-lawyer-set-replace-3000-employees-sberbank/.

[104] "Russian Oil Workers of the Near Future to Be Supervised by AI Systems." Sputnik International. October 19, 2019. https://sputniknews.com/business/201910191077095395-russian-oil-workers-of-the-near-future-to-be-supervised-by-ai-systems/.

[105] Atherton, Kelsey D. "Robots Will Replace Soldiers In Combat, Says Russia." Forbes. April 30, 2020. https://www.forbes.com/sites/kelseyatherton/2020/04/30/robots-will-replace-soldiers-in-combat-says-russia/?sh=546e3bc43c71.

[106] "Automation May Push 20M Russians Into Unemployment, Study Says." The Moscow Times. September 10, 2019. https://www.themoscowtimes.com/2019/09/10/automation-may-push-20-m-russians-unemployement-study-says-a67227.

[107] "The Outer Space Treaty." United Nations. https://www.unoosa.org/oosa/en/ourwork/spacelaw/treaties/introouterspacetreaty.html.

[108] "Russia Plans to Build Lunar Base after 2025." Xinhua. November 25, 2019. http://www.xinhuanet.com/english/2019-11/25/c_138582504.htm.

[109] Jones, Andrew. "China, Russia to Cooperate on Lunar Orbiter, Landing Missions." SpaceNews. September 19, 2019. https://spacenews.com/china-russia-to-cooperate-on-lunar-orbiter-landing-missions/.

[110] Oberhaus, Daniel. "The US Hitches Its Final Ride to Space From Russia-for Now." Wired. April 08, 2020. https://www.wired.com/story/the-us-hitches-its-final-ride-to-space-from-russia-for-now/.

[111] Chaudhury, Dipanjan Roy. "Russia to Share Critical Technology for India's Gaganyaan Project; Assist Entry into International Space Station." The Economic Times. July 12, 2019. https://economictimes.indiatimes.com/news/politics-and-nation/russia-to-share-critical-technology-for-indias-gaganyaan-project-assist-entry-into-intl-space-station/articleshow/70194179.cms?from=mdr.

[112] Chow, Denise. "This Russian Startup Wants to Put Huge Ads in Space. Not Everyone Is on Board with the Idea." NBCNews.com. January 19, 2019. https://www.nbcnews.com/mach/science/startup-wants-put-huge-ads-space-not-everyone-board-idea-ncna960296.

[113] Forrester, Chris. "Russia Block Means OneWeb Faces Extra-tough Challenge." IBC. August 16, 2019. https://www.ibc.org/trends/russia-block-means-oneweb-faces-extra-tough-challenge/4309.article.

[114] "Russia Plans to Become World Leader in Artificial Intelligence, Says PM." TASS. October 20, 2020. https://tass.com/economy/1214315.

[115] "Russia Sets up Lab to Create Quantum Computer." Xinhua. November 25, 2020. http://www.xinhuanet.com/english/2020-11/25/c_139542572.htm.

Chapter Six: China And The US Fight To Lead The World

[116] Aamir, Humza. "China to Replace All Foreign Hardware and Software at Government and Public Institutions by 2022." TechSpot. December 09, 2019. https://www.techspot.com/news/83088-china-replace-all-foreign-hardware-software-government-public.html.

[117] "Huawei HarmonyOS Powers the Latest Midea Smart Home Products." Gizmochina. November 11, 2020. https://www.gizmochina.com/2020/11/11/huawei-harmonyos-midea-smart-home-products/.

[118] Borak, Masha. "BYD's New Electric Car Has 5G and Runs Huawei Software." South China Morning Post. July 14, 2020. https://www.scmp.com/abacus/news-

bites/article/3093077/byds-new-5g-equipped-electric-car-runs-huawei-harmonyos-car.

[119] "Huawei Launches Its Own Mobile Operating System on Handsets." Al Jazeera. June 02, 2021. https://www.aljazeera.com/economy/2021/6/2/huawei-launches-its-own-mobile-operating-system-on-handsets.

[120] Christensen, Colin Peebles. "Africa Calling: How Transsion Rose to Dominate the African Phone Market." CKGSB. December 03, 2018. https://knowledge.ckgsb.edu.cn/2018/12/03/technology/africa-transsion-african-phone-market/.

[121] LeBlanc, Paul, and Maegan Vazquez. "Trump Orders TikTok's Chinese-owned Parent Company to Divest Interest in US Operations." CNN. August 15, 2020. https://www.cnn.com/2020/08/14/politics/tiktok-trump-executive-order/index.html.

[122] "China's SenseTime to Help Build $1bn AI Park in Malaysia." News - GCR. April 30, 2019. https://www.globalconstructionreview.com/news/chinas-sensetime-help-build-1bn-ai-park-malaysia/.

[123] Yushuo, Zhang. "China's Sogou, Abu Dhabi Media to Launch World's First Arabic AI News Anchor." Yicai Global. May 06, 2019.

https://www.yicaiglobal.com/news/china-sogou-abu-dhabi-media-to-launch-world-first-arabic-ai-news-anchor.

[124] Witze, Alexandra. "GPS Is Doing More Than You Thought." Scientific American. October 30, 2019. https://www.scientificamerican.com/article/gps-is-doing-more-than-you-thought/.

[125] Xie, John. "China's Rival to GPS Navigation Carries Big Risks." Voice of America. July 08, 2020. https://www.voanews.com/east-asia-pacific/voa-news-china/chinas-rival-gps-navigation-carries-big-risks.

[126] Meiping, Guo, and Li Qian. "Official: BeiDou System Products Exported to over 120 Countries and Regions." CGTN. August 05, 2020. https://news.cgtn.com/news/2020-08-03/BeiDou-system-products-exported-to-over-120-countries-and-regions--SEgZBfr1mM/index.html.

[127] Tsunashima, Toru. "In 165 Countries, China's Beidou Eclipses American GPS." Nikkei Asia. November 25, 2020. https://asia.nikkei.com/Spotlight/Century-of-Data/In-165-countries-China-s-Beidou-eclipses-American-GPS.

[128] Page, Jeremy, Kate O'Keeffe, and Rob Taylor. "Explained: US, China's Undersea Battle for Control of Global Internet Grid." Business Standard. July 09, 2019.

https://www.business-standard.com/article/international/explained-us-china-s-undersea-battle-for-control-of-global-internet-grid-119031300168_1.html.

[129] Packham, Colin. "Ousting Huawei, Australia Finishes Laying Undersea Internet Cable for Pacific Allies." Reuters. August 28, 2019. https://www.reuters.com/article/us-australia-pacific-cable-idUSKCN1VI08H.

[130] Delbert, Caroline. "Spies Could Steal Our Data From an 8,000-Mile Undersea Cable." Popular Mechanics. February 03, 2021. https://www.popularmechanics.com/science/a32960088/undersea-cable-hong-kong-data/.

[131] Harris, Mark. "Google and Facebook Turn Their Backs on Undersea Cable to China." TechCrunch. February 06, 2020. https://techcrunch.com/2020/02/06/google-and-facebook-turn-their-backs-on-undersea-cable-to-china/.

[132] "China Launches World's First Quantum Science Satellite." Physics World. September 28, 2017. https://physicsworld.com/a/china-launches-worlds-first-quantum-science-satellite/.

[133] Nowakowski, Tomasz. "China's 'Micius' Satellite Demonstrates Intercontinental Quantum Key Distribution for the First Time." SpaceFlight Insider. January 22, 2018. https://www.spaceflightinsider.com/organizations/china-national-space-administration/chinas-micius-satellite-demonstrates-intercontinental-quantum-key-distribution-first-time/.

[134] "China's Quantum Satellite Links with World's First Mobile Ground Station." Xinhua. January 02, 2020. http://www.xinhuanet.com/english/2020-01/02/c_138674381.htm.

[135] Jarman, Sam. "Quantum Connection Is Made by Flying Drones." Physics World. January 23, 2021. https://physicsworld.com/a/quantum-connection-is-made-by-flying-drones/.

[136] Elegant, Naomi Xu. "China Is Testing Its Digital Currency on a New Platform-with 500 Million Users." Fortune. July 08, 2020. https://fortune.com/2020/07/08/china-digital-currency-didi/.

[137] "China To Conduct Third Test Of Digital Yuan." PYMNTS.com. February 08, 2021.

https://www.pymnts.com/digital-payments/2021/china-to-conduct-third-test-drive-of-digital-yuan-currency/.

[138] Kharpal, Arjun. "China to Hand out $6.2 Million in Digital Currency to Beijing Residents as Part of Trial." CNBC. June 02, 2021. https://www.cnbc.com/2021/06/02/china-digital-currency-beijing-to-hand-out-6point2-million-in-trial.html.

[139] Liu, Coco, Dong Cao, Zheping Huang, and Thomas Seal. "Chinese Ride-Sharing Giant Didi Plans Entry Into Europe." Bloomberg.com. February 24, 2021. https://www.bloomberg.com/news/articles/2021-02-24/chinese-ride-sharing-giant-didi-plans-entry-into-western-europe.

[140] Mcdonald, Joe. "China Launches STAR, Tech Stock Market to Boost Industry." AP NEWS. July 18, 2019. https://apnews.com/article/d36c0345af7048f0b8431d8415c408cc.

[141] Kharpal, Arjun, and Ryan Browne. "Jack Ma's Ant Group Files for Hong Kong-Shanghai IPO, Says First-half Profit Rose 1,000%." CNBC. August 25, 2020. https://www.cnbc.com/2020/08/25/jack-mas-ant-group-files-for-hong-kong-shanghai-ipo.html.

[142] "Ant Group's IPO Sees Record $3 Trillion in Retail Demand." The Economic Times. October 31, 2021. https://economictimes.indiatimes.com/markets/ipos/fpos/ant-groups-ipo-sees-record-3-trillion-in-retail-demand/articleshow/78965668.cms?from=mdr.

[143] Kharpal, Arjun. "Alibaba Shares Dive 7% as Ant Group's Record $34.5 Billion IPO Is Suspended." CNBC. November 04, 2020. https://www.cnbc.com/2020/11/03/ant-group-ipo-in-shanghai-suspended.html.

[144] Fioretti, Julia. "Baidu Raises $3.1 Billion From Second Listing in Hong Kong." Bloomberg.com. March 17, 2021. https://www.bloomberg.com/news/articles/2021-03-17/baidu-is-said-poised-to-raise-3-1-billion-in-hong-kong-offering.

[145] Matlack, Carol. "Swift Justice: One Way to Make Putin Howl." Bloomberg.com. September 04, 2014. https://www.bloomberg.com/news/articles/2014-09-04/ultimate-sanction-barring-russian-banks-from-swift-money-system.

[146] Ostroukh, Andrey, and Elena Fabrichnaya. "Russia Backs Global Use of Its Alternative SWIFT System." Reuters. March 19, 2019.

https://www.reuters.com/article/russia-banks-swift-idUSL8N2163BU.

[147] Davda, Jignesh. "China, Russia & India Push Forward on SWIFT Alternative." Yahoo! Finance. November 29, 2019. https://finance.yahoo.com/news/china-russia-india-push-forward-102044240.html.

[148] Okuda, Koji. "China's Global Yuan Push Makes Inroads in Asia and Africa." Nikkei Asia. August 25, 2020. https://asia.nikkei.com/Business/Finance/China-s-global-yuan-push-makes-inroads-in-Asia-and-Africa.

[149] Zhu, Julie. "Exclusive: Huawei to Sell Phone Unit for $15 Billion to Shenzhen Government, Digital China, Others - Sources." Reuters. November 10, 2020. https://www.reuters.com/article/us-huawei-m-a-digital-china-exclusive-idUKKBN27Q0HB.

[150] Manekar, Sameer. "Chipmaker SMIC Inks $7.6 Billion Investment Deal for Wafer Production." Reuters. July 31, 2020. https://www.reuters.com/article/us-china-smic-semiconductor-idUSKCN24W2D6.

[151] He, Laura. "China Is Investing Billions in Chipmaking to Close the Gap with Its Global Rivals." CNN. July 07, 2020. https://www.cnn.com/2020/07/07/tech/smic-chinese-chipmaker-shanghai-intl-hnk/index.html.

[152] Ting-Fang, Cheng. "China Hires over 100 TSMC Engineers in Push for Chip Leadership." Nikkei Asia. August 12, 2020. https://asia.nikkei.com/Business/China-tech/China-hires-over-100-TSMC-engineers-in-push-for-chip-leadership.

[153] Barrett, Eamon. "China Will Spend $300 Billion on Semiconductor Imports as U.S. Squeezes Chip Supply." Fortune. August 27, 2020. https://fortune.com/2020/08/27/china-semiconductor-chip-imports-us-ban-huawei/.

[154] Jing, Meng. "Chinese Tech Companies Said to Be Shaping UN Facial Recognition Rules." South China Morning Post. December 02, 2019. https://www.scmp.com/tech/policy/article/3040164/chinese-tech-companies-are-shaping-un-facial-recognition-standards.

Chapter Seven: Unshackling Of Japan

[155] Westcott, Ben, and Yoko Wakatsuki. "Japan's Defense Ministry Asks for Decades-high 8.3% Budget Increase amid Growing Threats in East Asia." CNN. September 30, 2020. https://www.cnn.com/2020/09/30/asia/japan-military-budget-2020-intl-hnk/index.html.

[156] "Japan Defence Plan Counting on AI Tech Boost Amid Personnel Shortage - Reports." Sputnik International. November 20, 2018. https://sputniknews.com/military/201811201069968572-japan-defence-plan-ai-tech/.

[157] Ryall, Julian. "Japan Making 'pre-crime' AI to Predict Money Laundering, Terror Attacks." South China Morning Post. August 31, 2018. https://www.scmp.com/news/asia/east-asia/article/2162239/japan-developing-pre-crime-artificial-intelligence-predict-money.

[158] Brown, Mike. "Japan JASDF Wants Drones Fighting Alongside Air Force by the 2030s." Inverse. October 06, 2016. https://www.inverse.com/article/21828-japan-jasdf-drones-air-force-fighter-pilots-f-3.

[159] Kato, Masaya. "Japan Steps up Deployment of Defense AI and Robots." Nikkei Asia. January 27, 2019. https://asia.nikkei.com/Politics/Japan-steps-up-deployment-of-defense-AI-and-robots.

[160] Siddiqui, Huma. "India and Japan to Co-develop Unmanned Ground Vehicles, Robotics and Artificial Intelligence." The Financial Express. October 26, 2018. https://www.financialexpress.com/defence/india-

and-japan-to-co-develop-unmanned-ground-vehicles-robotics-and-artificial-intelligence/1362502/.

[161] Alpeyev, Pavel, and Takahiko Hyuga. "SoftBank's Son Makes a Pitch for Japan-Led Asia AI Superpower." Bloomberg.com. December 16, 2019. https://www.bloomberg.com/news/articles/2019-12-17/softbank-s-son-makes-a-pitch-for-japan-led-asia-ai-superpower.

[162] Sasaki, Susumu. "How Japan Plans to Build an Orbital Solar Farm." IEEE Spectrum: Technology, Engineering, and Science News. April 24, 2014. https://spectrum.ieee.org/green-tech/solar/how-japan-plans-to-build-an-orbital-solar-farm.

[163] McCurry, Justin. "Japan Will Become Carbon Neutral by 2050, PM Pledges." The Guardian. October 26, 2020. https://www.theguardian.com/world/2020/oct/26/japan-will-become-carbon-neutral-by-2050-pm-pledges.

[164] Baculinao, Eric. "China Unveils Proposal for $50 Trillion Global Electricity Network." NBCNews.com. March 31, 2016. https://www.nbcnews.com/business/energy/china-unveils-proposal-50-trillion-global-electricity-network-n548376.

[165] Pamuk, Humeyra, and Andrea Shalal. "Trump Administration Pushing to Rip Global Supply Chains from China: Officials." Reuters. May 04, 2020. https://www.reuters.com/article/us-health-coronavirus-usa-china-idUSKBN22G0BZ.

[166] "Japan Aims to Break Supply Chain Dependence on China in Light of COVID-19." The Japan Times. May 07, 2020. https://www.japantimes.co.jp/news/2020/03/06/business/japan-aims-break-supply-chain-dependence-china/.

[167] "Japan Reveals 87 Projects Eligible for 'China Exit' Subsidies." Nikkei Asia. July 17, 2020. https://asia.nikkei.com/Economy/Japan-reveals-87-projects-eligible-for-China-exit-subsidies.

[168] "Japan Offers $221 Million as 'China-exit' Subsidy for Japanese Companies." Business Insider. September 14, 2020. https://www.businessinsider.in/international/news/japan-offers-221-million-as-china-exit-subsidy-for-japanese-companies/articleshow/78103567.cms.

[169] "Over 40% of Japan Tech Firms Eyeing Shift from Reliance on China." The Japan Times. December 30, 2020.

https://www.japantimes.co.jp/news/2020/12/30/business/japan-tech-firms-china/.

[170] "Over 80% of Japan Inc. Recast Supply Chains as Pandemic Hit: Survey." Nikkei Asia. April 02, 2021. https://asia.nikkei.com/Business/Business-trends/Over-80-of-Japan-Inc.-recast-supply-chains-as-pandemic-hit-survey.

[171] Parama, Mardika. "Seven Companies to Relocate Facilities to Indonesia, Invest $850m." The Jakarta Post. June 30, 2020. https://www.thejakartapost.com/news/2020/06/30/seven-companies-to-relocate-facilities-to-indonesia-invest-850m.html.

[172] "Fanuc Plans Biggest Investment in China to Expand Robot Plant." Caixin Global. March 22, 2021. https://www.caixinglobal.com/2021-03-22/fanuc-plans-biggest-investment-in-china-to-expand-robot-plant-101678515.html.

[173] Singh, Manish. "Sony Invests $400M in Chinese Entertainment Platform Bilibili." TechCrunch. April 09, 2020. https://techcrunch.com/2020/04/09/sony-invests-400m-in-chinese-entertainment-platform-bilibili/.

[174] Shimono, Yuta. "Shionogi to Leverage Ping An Health Care Data to Speed Growth." Nikkei Asia. November 05, 2020. https://asia.nikkei.com/Business/Pharmaceuticals/Shionogi-to-leverage-Ping-An-health-care-data-to-speed-growth.

[175] Ogawa, Manami. "Tencent Helps Toyota Fix Security Vulnerabilities in Lexus NX300." Nikkei Asia. November 03, 2020. https://asia.nikkei.com/Business/Technology/Tencent-helps-Toyota-fix-security-vulnerabilities-in-Lexus-NX300.

[176] Hiramoto, Nobutaka, and Tsubasa Suruga. "As Japan Ponders Data Rules, 40% of Financial Firms Send User Info Overseas." Nikkei Asia. May 27, 2021. https://asia.nikkei.com/Business/Finance/As-Japan-ponders-data-rules-40-of-financial-firms-send-user-info-overseas.

[177] Suzuki, Wataru. "Line Cuts off Access from China to Protect Personal Data in Japan." Nikkei Asia. March 23, 2021. https://asia.nikkei.com/Business/Technology/Line-cuts-off-access-from-China-to-protect-personal-data-in-Japan.

[178] Nyabiage, Jevans. "China's Dominance of Rare Earths Supply Is a Concern in the West." South China Morning

Post. April 25, 2021.
https://www.scmp.com/news/china/diplomacy/article/3130990/chinas-dominance-rare-earths-supply-growing-concern-west.

179 Ryall, Julian. "Japan Moves to Secure Rare Earths to Reduce Dependence on China." South China Morning Post. August 17, 2020. https://www.scmp.com/week-asia/politics/article/3097672/japan-moves-secure-rare-earths-reduce-dependence-china.

180 Berke, Jeremy. "Japan Discovered a Rare-Earth Mineral Deposit This Year That Can Supply The World For Centuries." ScienceAlert. December 30, 2018.
https://www.sciencealert.com/japan-discovered-a-rare-earth-mineral-deposit-that-can-supply-the-world-for-centuries.

Chapter Eight: The Israeli North Star

181 Al-Khalidi, Suleiman. "Middle East Drought a Threat to Global Food Prices." Reuters. March 07, 2014.
https://www.reuters.com/article/us-climate-drought-middleast-idUSBREA2611P20140307.

182 Kartin, Amnon. "Water Scarcity Problems in Israel." GeoJournal. March 2001.

https://link.springer.com/article/10.1023/A:1019590029553

[183] "How Desalination Came to the Rescue in Israel." ISI Water. March 14, 2017. https://isi-water.com/desalination-rescues-israel/.

[184] Rabinovitch, Ari. "Israel Receives Bids for Seventh Desalination Plant." Reuters. August 06, 2020. https://ca.reuters.com/article/idUSKCN2521XU.

[185] Kolyohin, Nick. "Feature: Israel Aims to Secure All of Its Water Supply through Desalination." Xinhua. November 22, 2019. http://www.xinhuanet.com/english/2019-11/22/c_138575940.htm.

[186] "Israeli Tech Company Develops AI Robotic Beehive." Xinhua. July 20, 2020. http://www.xinhuanet.com/english/2020-07/21/c_139227490.htm.

[187] Millis, Joe. "Israeli Biotech Boffins Cook up Algae Falafel to Feed the World." The Times of Israel. January 02, 2019. https://jewishnews.timesofisrael.com/israeli-biotech-whizzes-cook-up-algae-falafel-to-feed-the-world/.

[188] Solomon, Shoshanna. "Biotech Firm in Israel Makes Fertility Waves with Genetically Modified Hormone." The

Times of Israel. August 09, 2018. https://www.timesofisrael.com/biotech-firm-in-israel-makes-fertility-waves-with-genetically-modified-hormone/.

[189] "Israeli Biotech Firm's ALS Treatment Shows Positive Results in Trials." The Jerusalem Post | JPost.com. August 05, 2020. https://www.jpost.com/health-science/israeli-biotech-firms-als-treatment-shows-positive-results-in-trials-637521.

[190] "Israeli Biotech Firm Successfully Reverses Human Bone Loss in Early Trial." The Jerusalem Post. December 07, 2016. https://www.jpost.com/business-and-innovation/tech/israeli-biotech-firm-successfully-reverses-human-bone-loss-in-early-trial-474686.

[191] "Israel to Build 1st Biotechnology Plant Producing New AIDS Drug." Belta. October 24, 2018. https://eng.belta.by/society/view/israel-to-build-1st-biotechnology-plant-producing-new-aids-drug-115948-2018/.

[192] LaVito, Angelica. "Israeli Company That Claims Cure for Cancer Would Face Years of Testing Ahead for US Market - Even If It Works." CNBC. January 29, 2019. https://www.cnbc.com/2019/01/29/israeli-company-that-claims-cancer-cure-faces-skeptical-us-market.html.

[193] Zonshine, Idan. "Israeli Start-ups Team up to Make Epi Genetic Mega-cannabis." The Jerusalem Post. January 13, 2020. https://www.jpost.com/health-science/israeli-start-ups-team-up-to-make-genetically-modified-mega-cannabis-613792.

[194] Liao, Shannon. "The Marshall Islands Replaces the US Dollar with Its Own Cryptocurrency." The Verge. May 23, 2018.

https://www.theverge.com/2018/5/23/17384608/marshall-islands-cryptocurrency-us-dollar-usd-currency.

[195] "Israeli Company Partners with Marshall Islands to Launch Digital Currency." The Times of Israel. March 09, 2019. https://www.timesofisrael.com/israeli-company-partners-with-marshall-islands-to-launch-digital-currency/.

[196] Solomon, Shoshanna. "In 'first,' Delivery Drone Gets to Destination in Israel without GPS Signal." The Times of Israel. February 10, 2021.

https://www.timesofisrael.com/in-first-delivery-drone-gets-to-destination-in-israel-without-gps-signal/.

[197] Doffman, Zak. "Israeli Military Launches Radical New Google Maps Alternative." Forbes. June 30, 2020.

https://www.forbes.com/sites/zakdoffman/2020/06/30/j

ust-like-google-maps-secret-israeli-military-unit-launches-radical-new-app/?sh=10396b9b7c9b.

198 Reich, Aaron. "Bar-Ilan's On-chip Memory Tech Ranks in Top 3 Ventures in Swiss Contest." The Jerusalem Post. July 31, 2020. https://www.jpost.com/jpost-tech/bar-ilans-on-chip-memory-tech-ranks-in-top-3-ventures-in-swiss-contest-636915.

199 Freund, Karl. "World-Record AI Chip Announced By Habana Labs." Forbes. June 20, 2019. https://www.forbes.com/sites/moorinsights/2019/06/20/world-record-ai-chip-announced-by-habana-labs/?sh=65e74f7c6c06.

200 "Intel Announces First AI Chip Developed in Israel." CTECH. August 20, 2019. https://www.calcalistech.com/ctech/articles/0,7340,L-3768662,00.html.

201 "Nvidia Taps Into Israel's Talent With New AI Research Center." NoCamels. October 21, 2018. https://nocamels.com/2018/10/nvidia-israel-ai-research-center/.

202 Schindler, Max. "Chinese Millionaire to Set up Artificial Intelligence Lab in Haifa." The Jerusalem Post. September 23, 2017. https://www.jpost.com/israel-news/chinese-

millionaire-to-set-up-artificial-intelligence-lab-in-haifa-505742.

[203] Solomon, Shoshanna. "Israel's Cortica Seeks to Nip at Mobileye's Heels with Brain-mimicking Tech." The Times of Israel. April 21, 2019. https://www.timesofisrael.com/israels-cortica-seeks-to-nip-at-mobileye-heels-with-brain-mimicking-tech/.

[204] Solomon, Shoshanna. "Intel to Buy Mobileye for $15.3 Billion in Largest Purchase of Israeli Tech." The Times of Israel. March 13, 2017. https://www.timesofisrael.com/intel-said-to-buy-israels-mobileye-for-up-to-16-billion/.

[205] Yi, Ding. "Chinese Truckmaker and Israeli Sensor Firm Team Up on Self-Driving Trucks." Caixin Global. February 13, 2020. https://www.caixinglobal.com/2020-02-13/chinese-truckmaker-and-israeli-sensor-firm-team-up-on-self-driving-trucks-101514888.html.

[206] Ravid, Barak. "U.S. Warns Chinese Investments in Israeli Tech Industry Could Pose Security Threat." Axios. December 21, 2020. https://www.axios.com/chinese-investment-israeli-tech-1c9dad9e-bbe2-456e-8651-ff7e08bd3f66.html.

[207] Williams, Dan, and Rami Ayyub. "Israel, U.S. near Deal to Exclude China from Israeli 5G Networks: U.S. Official." Reuters. August 14, 2020. https://www.reuters.com/article/us-israel-usa-5g-china-idUSKCN25A2CF.

Notes

Notes

Made in the USA
Columbia, SC
08 November 2021

48560434R00133